OTHELLO

William Shakespeare

OTHELLO

Emma Smith

NORTHCOTE
BRITISH COUNCIL

© Copyright 2005 by Emma Smith

First published in 2005 by Northcote House Publishers Ltd, Horndon House, Horndon, Devon PL19 9NQ, United Kingdom.
Tel: +44 (01822) 810066 Fax: +44 (01822) 810034.

British Library Cataloguing-in-Publication Data
A catalogue record for this book is available from the British Library

ISBN 0-7463-1082-X hardcover
ISBN 0-7463-0999-6 paperback

Typeset by PDQ Typesetting, Newcastle-under-Lyme
Printed and bound in the United Kingdom
by Athenaeum Press Ltd., Gateshead, Tyne & Wear

Contents

List of Illustrations   vi

Acknowledgements   vii

References   viii

Introduction   1

1   Doubleness   4

2   Race and *Othello*   28

3   The Domestic Sphere   49

4   Tragedy and Comedy   73

Notes   90

Select Bibliography   99

Index   102

Illustrations

1. Title page to 1622 quarto edition.   5
   Bodleian Library: Arch. G d.43 (7).

2. 'Peacham' drawing of *Titus Andronicus*   30
   (Longleat Portland Papers, If.159V).
   Reproduced by permission of the Marquess of Bath,
   Longleat House, Warminster, Wiltshire, Great Britain

3. Abdul El-Quahéd Ben Messasud, Moorish   33
   Ambassador to Queen Elizabeth I.
   The University of Birmingham Collections.

Acknowledgements

The immediate stimulus for my work on this book was an Oxford University Summer School for Adults in 2002. My thanks are due to Betty Bettachi, Dagmar Gerstgrasser, Jennifer Gilby, Mike Hodgetts, Joyce Ligertwood, Budge Little, Marion Lupu, Jill Ashley Miller, Ann Peacocke and Noriko Shishido for their energizing engagement with *Othello*.

References

All references to Shakespeare's plays, including *Othello*, are taken from *William Shakespeare: The Complete Works*, ed. Stanley Wells and Gary Taylor (Oxford: Oxford University Press, 1986), unless otherwise indicated.

Where quotations from contemporary writers are cited from original texts, spelling has been modernized.

Introduction

When Iago, played by Kenneth Branagh, illustrates his game plan for his hapless victims in Oliver Parker's 1995 film of *Othello*, he is shown manipulating black-and-white chess pieces: the white Queen stands for Desdemona, the black King is Othello, and a white Knight on horseback serves as Cassio. In Jonathan Miller's BBC television film of 1981, the so-called temptation scene (3.3) is played in a large, bare interior space with a black-and-white chequerboard floor across which Iago moves Othello towards checkmate. In its combination of antagonism between black-and-white pieces, its requirement for cerebral plotting and its rewards for taking opportunistic advantage of an opponent's errors, chess might seem the obvious gaming metaphor for *Othello*.

But there is a more immediate parallel I want to suggest, as particularly, perhaps serendipitously, apposite for the themes and procedures of this complex play. In 1968 'Reversi', a popular nineteenth-century game 'of territorial occupation involving placement and capture but not movement', was rebranded and relaunched by a Japanese toy company. The game requires the capture of the opponent's pieces 'by enclosure and conversion':[1] double-sided counters, red and black in the original version and now recast in black and white, mean that the pieces can be turned to show either colour depending on which player has captured them. The new name for this game was 'Othello'.

Why this game of capture and reversal was given this name at this particular historical juncture is open to speculation. While Shakespeare's *Othello* does not appear to have been particularly prominent in Japanese culture during the 1960s – indeed, it has been argued that its racial politics are incomprehensible in Japan[2] – the choice may have been influenced by the wide-

1

spread publicity for John Dexter's National Theatre production of the play in 1964, directed by Stuart Burge the following year on film, with Laurence Olivier as the Moor. Another, darker contemporaneity haunts the decision: 1968 was a year of particular racial tensions, with the assassination of the American civil-rights leader Martin Luther King in Memphis, Tennessee, and global coverage of the racialized nature of American society; in Britain, the right-wing politician Enoch Powell delivered his infamous 'rivers of blood' speech decrying immigration and calling for repatriation. But whatever the connection, the game 'Othello' can serve as a stimulating metaphor for the play itself. Both play and game are simultaneously dependent on absolute binary distinctions – between the two colours black and white, between Venice and Turkey, between men and women – and on the fact that the 'two-faced', or, as Iago might have it, Janus-faced, counters can and do shift from one to the other. Like its namesake game of double-sided counters, *The Tragedy of Othello, The Moor of Venice* is immediately marked by doubleness. The play's double title establishes a theme of duplication and paradox that, this study will argue, is a crucial ongoing aspect of the play's language and structure.

The play's careful anatomizing of boundary disputes between self and other, Venetian and Turk, man and woman, home and abroad, black and white, insider and outsider is its key theme, giving it an overriding structure we might term 'agonistic', from the Greek for contest or struggle. The first chapter in this study is concerned with aspects of doubleness, substitution and duplication. Chapter 2 considers the black-and-white polarity embodied in the marriage of Desdemona and Othello and the consequences of Othello's outsider status, both in the context of the play's first audiences and at other historical and cultural junctures too. In Chapter 3, the issue of the domestic and its relation to the exotic is discussed as part of a gendered spatial discourse that the play articulates and sabotages. Chapter 4 engages the hybrid generic status of a tragic play with many comic cognates. Throughout these particular interpretative foci we see the play attempting to manage boundaries and distinctions, working to establish a binary and to maintain it against dissolution. This study will explore how the tensile oxymoric fabric of *The Tragedy of Othello, the Moor of Venice* is stretched to breaking point and culminates in the self-destruction of its eponymous, and eponymously divided, hero.

1

Doubleness

Reading *Othello* involves the immediate engagement with a paradox. When it was first published in 1622, the play was titled *The Tragedy of Othello*, with the prominent subtitle *The Moor of Venice*. This publication, known as the quarto text, sometimes abbreviated in critical discussions to Q1 ('quarto' refers to the size of book, made from paper folded twice to make four leaves, and therefore measuring about 22 × 16 cm), uses the double title on the title page and as a running title across the headers to each page, thus keeping both parts of the double title in view throughout the play (Fig. 1). Again in the collected First Folio, or F text, of Shakespeare's plays published a year later in 1623 ('folio' also refers to the book size, this time a prestigious format in which the paper was folded only once to make a book of about 45 × 32 cm), *Othello* is the only play to have a split or double title running across verso and recto leaves.

Both the fact of the play's double title and the syntax of its subtitle stress doubleness, and it is the preposition 'of' that particularly activates *Othello*'s central paradox. A Moor – literally a black man from North Africa – cannot ever be 'of' Venice. We need only look at the title of an earlier Shakespeare play, *The Merchant of Venice*, where it is crucial to the plot that the eponymous character Antonio, unlike his Jewish adversary Shylock, is a Venetian, 'of Venice', to see how different these two uses of 'of' are. In fact the preposition 'of' has two ambiguous meanings in the early modern period. One, waning sense is 'from, away from, out of' (*OED* I.1.), and suggests the idea of expulsion retained in the modern spelling 'off'. This disconnective sense, in which 'of' indicates separation or distance from, is being replaced by a contradictory meaning stressing affiliation, 'indicating the thing, or person whence

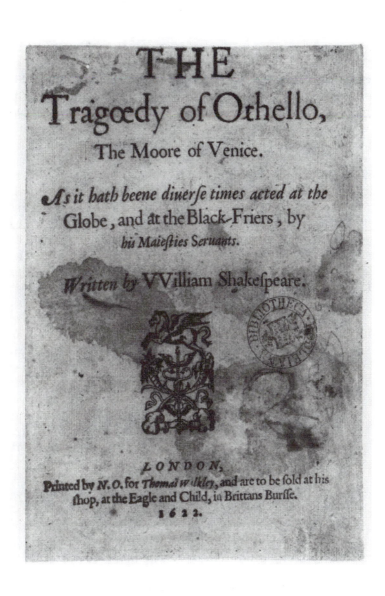

Figure 1. Title page to the 1622 quarto edition.

anything originates, comes, is acquired or sought' (*OED* III), with a particular stress on 'racial or local origin' (9). Thus the historical meanings of 'of' register the sense in which Othello both belongs to and is rejected by the Venice he simultaneously serves and threatens. He is both 'of' and 'off' Venice. As this study will discuss, Othello's peculiar status as insider and outsider to Venice – 'of' in both its early modern meanings – means that he and his marriage embody the system of assailed and confounded binary oppositions on which the play is structured. 'The Moor of Venice' thus opens the play with an immediate semantic and ontological impossibility. In rhetorical terms, 'Moor of Venice' registers as an oxymoron (a figure of speech yoking together two apparently contradictory parts); in psychic terms, we could see Othello's curious and insistent agname as a figure for the dividedness or alienation that is the play's governing dynamic.

This initial figure of doubleness or paradox continues. Iago's description of a 'civil monster' (4.1.62) is another oxymoron, as is Othello's 'honourable murderer' (5.2.300). It soon becomes clear to the audience that the oft-repeated 'honest Iago' or 'good Iago' is an ironic or concealed paradox, since Iago is far from either good or honest. So too is 'ocular proof' (3.3.365), in which what is seen is no proof at all. Oxymoron functions as a condensed form of doubt or contradiction – a syntactically distilled version of Othello's cauterized anguish at Iago's insinuations: 'I think my wife be honest, and think she is not./ I think that thou art just, and think thou art not' (3.3.389–90).

In addition to these repeated oxymorons, another, less familiar rhetorical term – hendiadys – is also useful. Hendiadys (literally, from the Greek, 'one through two') was defined by the Renaissance rhetorician George Puttenham in 1589 as: 'yet another manner of speech when ye will seem to make two of one not thereunto constrained, which therefore we call the figure of Twins, the Greeks Endiadis thus' – or, as a modern dictionary of literary terms puts it, 'the use of two substantives ... joined by a conjunction, to express a single but complex idea: one of the elements is logically subordinate to the other'.[1] Examples from *Othello* might be 'the native act and figure of my heart' (1.1.62), 'flag and sign of love' (1.1.158), 'circumscription and confine' (1.2.27), 'engluts and swallows' (1.3.57), 'maimed and most imperfect' (1.3.99), 'stubborn and boisterous' (1.3.226–7) and 'downright violence and storm' (1.3.249). The crucial term in hendiadys, as these examples show, is the conjunction 'and': it is a figure of pairing and concurrence. Rather than working with an adjective + noun/ adverb + verb, hendiadys doubles up on identical parts of speech while maintaining their syntactical distinctness. Hendiadys is thus a kind of oxymoron without that figure's intrinsic antagonism; that is, hendiadys uses two terms as a form of duplication, rather than contradiction as in oxymoron. In his book *Shakespeare's Language*, Frank Kermode observes that the rhetorical figure of hendiadys is particularly prominent in the opening scenes of the play: all those examples listed above occur within the first act. As Kermode points out, examples of hendiadys become harder to find as *Othello* progresses and Shakespeare 'becomes less fond of semantic collision and contraction'.[2]

It is striking that these rhetorical figures involving doubling and conjunction should be so prominent in the scenes that establish the marriage of Othello and Desdemona, in that pre-play miniature romantic comedy of elopement and marriage that comprises the Venetian portion of *Othello*. Both the teleology and the ideology of that romantic comedy narrative emphasize a movement towards two becoming one through marriage. Perhaps, therefore, the distinctive rhetorical style of that section of *Othello* can be related to its themes – even as the couple are joined together through marriage, the language continues to stress separateness. In a comparable critical manœuvre, Kermode argues that the incidence of hendiadys in *Hamlet* is connected to that play's ambivalence to its themes of incest and adultery, of 'the conjunction of what is ordinarily disjunct'.[3] Here in *Hamlet* the language is working to keep distinct those relationships the play's themes have allowed to become confounded: that marriage of the 'uncle-father and aunt-mother' (2.2.376) in 'incestuous sheets' (1.2.157).

This connection between theme and language is even more apposite in the case of hendiadys in *Othello*. If the yoked repetitions of the figure of hendiadys serve at once to couple and to separate, then this figure of speech serves as a striking rhetorical microcosm of attitudes to the relationship of Othello and Desdemona. The first reference to the couple has them in a

7

physical hendiadys, making 'the beast with two backs' (1.1.118–19) in a lodging house bearing the inauspicious sign of that physical oxymoron Sagittary, or the half-man, half-beast mythological figure of the centaur. Iago's debased view of sexual congress sees in the newly-weds a monstrous coupling, the impossible partnership of two things that can and should never make one. The 'and' here, the syntactic fulcrum of the figure of hendiadys, is the debased pairing of Desdemona *and* Othello. Just as the 'and' in Iago's baleful admission 'I hate the Moor, And it is thought abroad that 'twixt my sheets/ He has done my office' (1.3.378-80), where 'And' signals not the expected causal connective 'because' or 'since' but merely a sequence of malevolent and unmotivated thoughts, the 'and' in hendiadys functions again in *Othello*, as in *Hamlet*, to keep distinct, to prise apart, and to indicate resistance to an incestuous or unorthodox sexuality.

In part, *Othello* is, or is predicated on, a familiar kind of love story, the tale of two people whose love triumphs over their material differences. The implications of this structure are discussed in more detail in Chapter 4, where they are considered as part of the play's extensive debt to different comedic antecedents. But, whereas the rhetoric of romantic love yearns towards absolute union, *Othello* continues to stress separateness. One of the prayers in use in the Elizabethan marriage ceremony used this common image of two being 'knitted' together in matrimony: 'it should never be lawful to put asunder those, whom Thou by matrimony hast made one'.[4] The idea of two separate individuals becoming one is a movement the play resists. In microcosm on a syntactic level as demonstrated in the prevalence of oxymoron and hendiadys, and writ large in *Othello's* plot on a practical level, these two never really do become one. Othello's readiness to believe his wife has been unfaithful, notwithstanding the fiendish psychological cleverness of Iago, could be seen as an index of the couple's fundamental separateness, the gulf between them, and their increasing failure of communication.

Thus the decline in frequency of hendiadys as a figure for imperfect, and perhaps impossible, union – for twinning rather than matrimony, a figure for two rather than one – corresponds to the gradual and seemingly inexorable opening of physical and emotional space between the married couple: the play thus picks up and magnifies the troubling linguistic separation intrinsic to the duplicative rhetoric of the opening act. Even, then, as the play's narrative seems most to confirm the marriage of Othello and Desdemona, its habitual turn of phrase seeks to undermine it. In his famous essay 'The *Othello* Music', G. Wilson Knight draws attention to something similar, arguing that the language of the play is characterized by its 'aloofness': 'the resultant of an inward aloofness of image from image, word from word. The dominant quality is separation, not, as is more usual in Shakespeare, cohesion'[5]. Juxtaposition and disjunction, rather than fusion, are thus the governing movements of the play's language, and this has important implications for its presentation of the transgressive relationship between Othello and Desdemona.

This sense that the language of the play is striving towards separation makes it the key vehicle for mirroring as well as enacting the split between its central couple. As Iago comforts Roderigo at the end of the first act, their 'violent commence-ment' is already marked with a movement towards 'answerable sequestration' (1.3.343–5). From the outset, the play is structured around frequent acts of separation or interjection: Othello is roused from his marital bed to attend the Senate in Act 1; sudden state demands take him from Venice to Cyprus; the couple travel to the island in separate vessels; their bed is disturbed again by the drinking bout in Act 2, Scene 3. As many critics have noted, every time the couple seem to withdraw offstage alone together, some extreme action is proposed to disturb them, to such an extent that some have questioned when, and if, the marriage is ever consummated. It is testament to the play's insistent but oblique eroticism that critics have been so singularly preoccupied with the question of whether and when the couple have sex: Michael Neill writes of one detailed essay entitled 'Othello's Unconsummated Marriage' that its authors 'become victims, like the hero himself, of the scopophile economy of this tragedy and prey to its voyeuristic excitements'.[6]

The couple, in fact, are very rarely alone together. Iago takes his cue for his masterly manipulation in Act 3, Scene 3 from the unexpected news that Cassio was a party to Othello's courtship 'from first to last ... and went between us very oft' (3.3.98–102), forcing a retrospective reassessment of the earlier accounts of the couple's meetings where no Cassio was mentioned. It could be argued that there were always three people in this marriage. Kenneth Burke describes Othello, Iago, and Desdemona forming 'a tragic trinity of ownership' as 'the three principles of possession [Desdemona], possessor [Othello] and estrangement (threat of loss) [Iago]'.[7] Interestingly, the posters for three different modern film adaptations of the play, the updated *O* directed by Tim Blake Nelson in 2001, the modern police force *Othello* written by Andrew Davies for the BBC in 2002 and Oliver Parker's 1995 film *Othello*, all imagine the psychosexual dynamic of the play as a triangle between the Othello, Desdemona and Iago figures. Here it is Iago, not the fallguy Cassio, who makes a crowd out of the company of Othello and Desdemona's relationship, and who embodies the real and insidious threat to their unity. In this light, Desdemona's euphemistic encouragement to her suitor, bidding him 'if I had a friend that loved her,/I should but teach him how to tell my story,/ And that would woo her' (1.3.163–5), looks like a presentiment of the crowdedness, actual and imagined, of their relationship, rather than a piece of innocent flirtation.

As Othello tries to hold onto the remnants of his faith in Desdemona, he remembers his belief that 'the world hath not a sweeter creature!' (4.1.179–180), but his elaboration of her value is of that of a courtesan: 'She might lie by an emperor's side, and command him tasks' (4.1.180–1). Even the perverse intimacy of the murder – the only time Othello and Desdemona are alone together on stage – is intruded on by Emilia's knocking, and her dying request 'lay me by my mistress' side' (5.2.244) establishes the scene of the death as an unexpected *ménage à trois* rather than a *liebestod* (from opera – an aria proclaiming the suicide of lovers, literally 'love's death'). The high-angle shot that concludes Parker's film of the play goes further in showing all four – Desdemona, Othello, Emilia, and Iago – on the marital bed, emphasizing the parallel course of the two marriages. This structural principle of *interruptus*, a compulsive movement to intervene in moments of intimacy and to interpose additional and superfluous persons between the couple, is enacted at the semantic level also, through the use of these rhetorical devices of hendiadys and oxymoron.

10

In addition to these manœuvres by which the play's language and structure sabotage the relationship between Othello and Desdemona, keeping the couple separate and denying them the ecstasy of true union, *Othello* also moves towards fracturing the individual and dividing it into parts. A sense of self-alienation threatens almost all the characters; a lack of individual completeness haunts their lives. Thus Iago's sinister manifesto of duplicity, 'I am not what I am' (1.1.65), stands as only the most extreme version of a divided selfhood variously experienced throughout the play. Desdemona is described as 'beguiled ... of herself' (1.3.66); in losing his reputation, Cassio – the only character in the play to have two names – has lost 'the immortal part of myself' (2.3.257); Othello is brought from nobility to brutishness, such that his behaviour 'would not be believed in Venice' (4.1.242). It is, of course, a commonplace of *Othello* criticism to discuss Iago's infiltration of Othello's nobility of speech with his own brutish and base diction. This imagery of sexual disgust infects the idealized and romantic music of Othello's rhetoric. Polish theatre director Jan Kott identifies the two characters as embodying quite different philosophical perspectives:

> Says Iago: The world consists of villains and fools; of those who devour and those who are devoured. People are like animals; they copulate and eat each other. The weak do not deserve pity, they are just as abominable, only more stupid than the strong. The world is vile. Says Othello: The world is beautiful and people are noble. There exist in it love and loyalty.

In the matter of Desdemona's fidelity, Kott argues that what is at stake is nothing less than 'a dispute on the nature of the world'.[8] The man who can discourse on 'moving accidents by flood and field' (1.3.134), deploying with exquisite precision unfamiliar words such as 'antres' (1.3.139) and 'agnize' (1.3.230), is reduced to the stuttering prose bestiality of 'Pish! Noses, ears, and lips! Is't possible? Confess? Handkerchief? O devil!' (4.1.40–2). Like Iago, Othello begins to talk in the gutteral monosyllables of sexual loathing, as the contamination of his mind is enacted through the degradation of his speech. The bestiary of the world as inhabited by Iago, populated with 'blind puppies', 'baboon' and 'guinea hen', takes over. Othello recognizes the effects of jealousy as 'exchange me for a goat' (3.3.184), and in linguistic terms this is what happens. With his exclamation 'goats and monkeys' (4.1.265) before the bewildered Venetian delegation, Othello's rhetorical transformation into Iago reaches its linguistic and moral nadir.

Jealousy may indeed be the only emotion really understood by the calculating and cold ensign. Writing of his preparation to play the role of Iago in Terry Hands's 1985 production for the Royal Shakespeare Company, David Suchet notes 'Iago represents Jealousy, is Jealousy', but advises, following Emilia's observation that the jealous 'are not ever jealous for the cause,/ But jealous for they're jealous' (3.4.157–8), 'don't look for reasons for the behaviour of jealous people'.[9] Shakespeare's major source for *Othello* is Giraldi Cinthio's collection of prose stories printed as *Hecatommithi* in 1565, but, whereas Cinthio's villain acts as he does entirely because he is 'ardently in love with Disdemona' and believes that she 'was in love with the Corporal [Cassio]', Iago's motives have been endlessly debated since Coleridge's mellifluous and oft-quoted assessment of 'the motive-hunting of a motiveless malignity'.[10] Iago does, however, offer at least two reasons for jealousy. At the outset of the play he is preoccupied by professional envy of Cassio's promotion, and later there is that almost casual allusion to sexual jealousy already quoted above (1.3.378–80). Jealousy is what Iago transmits to the general, even as he ironically urges him to beware it: 'the souls of all my tribe defend/ From jealousy!' (3.3.179–80).

Indeed, this transmission of jealousy, a kind of psychic equivalent of the ritual of blood fraternity with which Iago and Othello seal their pact to murder Desdemona in Parker's 1995 film, signals a way in which Iago and Othello function as mimetic doubles. In *Titus Andronicus* (*c*.1590) Shakespeare gives us a Moor character, Aaron, who partakes of both the sexual magnetism of Othello and the malignant plotting of Iago; again, in *The Winter's Tale* (1611), he gives us Leontes, an Othello who needs no Iago to bring himself to murderous jealousy through his own lurid imaginings. Both the earlier and the later Shakespearian plays suggest that, rather than being seen as psychologically complete and autonomous personages, Othello and Iago might seem to function as duplicates, or as a projection of an already fractured or doubled heroic psyche. On occasion actors have alternated the roles of Othello and Iago – as Henry Irving and Edwin Booth did in the nineteenth century or Richard Burton and John Neville did in the 1950s. When Hal Scott directed a black Othello (Avery Brooks) partnered by a black Iago (Andre Braugher) in Washington DC in 1990, he made the bond between the two men all the more comprehensible and tragic.[11] René Girard argues that 'Iago is the perfect confidant because he is Othello's mimetic double and therefore so close to him at times that the two men become each other's mirror image'.[12] We can see this in an extended quotation from Act 3, Scene 3, where they echo each other so as to form a fractured soliloquy of circling and recurrent suspicions that can neither be fully articulated nor fully suppressed:

IAGO.   Indeed?
OTHELLO.   Indeed? Ay, indeed. Discern'st thou aught in that?
Is he not honest?
IAGO.   Honest, my lord?
OTHELLO.   Honest? Ay, honest.
IAGO.   My lord, for aught I know.
OTHELLO.   What dost thou think?
IAGO.   Think, my lord?
OTHELLO.   'Think, my lord?' By heaven, thou echo'st me
As if there were some monster in thy thought
Too hideous to be shown!

(3.3.103–12)

In fact, this could be interpreted as projection: the monster is already and always in Othello's own thought. Or in Iago's: Janet Adelman argues that Iago 'can see his own darkness localized and reflected in Othello's blackness, or rather in what he makes – and teaches Othello to make – of Othello's blackness'.[13] Thus the relationship between the two men is one of perverse psychic mutuality or doubleness: Jonathan Miller's television version has Othello enter in Act 4 wearing Iago's leather doublet. Iago's strange line 'Were I the Moor I would not be Iago' (1.1.57) registers the uncanny interplay between them. Michael Mac Liammóir's memoir of the filming of Orson Welles's film of *Othello*, in which he played Iago, describes 'the growing dependence of Othello on Iago's presence, the merging of the two men into one murderous image like a pattern of loving shadows welded'.[14] There are other possible mirrorings and mergings, too. In a newspaper review of Jude Kelly's 1997 production, Lois Potter noted 'the growing sympathy between the two abused wives, as one comes to resemble the other':[15] the stage direction at 5.2.242 in the Quarto text reads 'Iago kils his wife', as if in conscious echo of Othello's crime moments earlier. If Iago personifies jealousy or suspicion, his projected tortures are the literalization of Othello's torments 'on the rack' (3.3.340). A revealing still reproduced in Julie Hankey's stage history of the play shows James Earl Jones as Othello in the 1982 New York production with Christopher Plummer as Iago: the perspective gives the impression that Iago is a tiny interior demon projected outwards, sitting at Othello's shoulder.[16]

Othello realizes that 'a hornèd man's a monster and a beast' (4.1.60), and Iago pushes home the point: 'There's many a beast then in a populous city,/ And many a civil monster' (4.1.61–2). Unsurprisingly it is the figure of oxymoron, that 'civil monster', with which he does so. When F. R. Leavis argued that Iago is 'not much more than a necessary piece of dramatic mechanism', he is arguing for Iago as a representative of something not entirely external to Othello himself: 'Iago's power, in fact, in the temptation-scene is that he represents something that is in Othello – in Othello the husband of Desdemona: the essential traitor is within the gates …. The tragedy is inherent in the Othello-Desdemona relation, and Iago is a mechanism necessary for precipitating tragedy in a dramatic action'.[17] Leavis's account of the play locates the seeds of destruction in the very relationship of Othello and Desdemona, thus offering a corrective, albeit an uncomfortably racially essentialist one, to readings of the play that stress Iago's machinations as the only source of agency.

There is a good deal of truth in a model of linguistic and moral degradation through the insidious verbal agency of Iago, but it is not the whole story. Perhaps the play, and its readers, have been over-inclined to scapegoat Iago as the fount and the motion of the destruction of Othello and Desdemona, without taking account of a more thoroughgoing and intrinsic textual prejudice against their relationship. The 1999 Macpherson report into the widespread failings of London's Metropolitan Police in investigating the murder of the black student Stephen Lawrence introduced to a bewildered and resistant British society the concept of 'institutional racism': 'the collective failure of an organisation to provide an appropriate and professional service to people because of their colour, culture, or ethnic origin. It can be seen or detected in processes, attitudes and behaviour which amount to discrimination through unwitting prejudice, ignorance, thoughtlessness and racist stereotyping which disadvantage minority ethnic people'.[18] It could be argued that that insidious and insistent movement of the language of *Othello* towards disjunction and separation – that sense in which two never fully become one – enacts at a syntactic level a fundamental thematic unease – an institutional or 'collective failure', in Macpherson's terms – around the central relationship of black Othello and white Desdemona. Hendiadys and oxymoron are rhetorical features of the language of the *play*, rather than of particular characters. The troubling fact that Iago is so successful in destroying their relationship may attest to his terrible ingenuity: it may also indicate that at some level the play is uncomfortable with the marriage.

It would, of course, have been possible to endorse the lovers' choices by showing their relationship weathering Iago's malice. But we are not afforded this comfort. Perhaps, with the Romantic poet Coleridge, the play registers that 'it would be something monstrous to conceive this beautiful Venetian girl falling in love with a veritable negro', or, like Charles Lamb, finds 'something extremely revolting in the courtship and wedded caresses of Othello and Desdemona', or shares what A. C. Bradley, with an unconsciously coercive use of the shared possessive, calls 'the aversion of our blood' to a 'coal-black' Othello. When one of the play's most sensitive recent editors, Norman Sanders, proposes that 'only a Negroid Othello can produce the desired responses in the theatres of the western world', we have to wonder whose desires are being perversely gratified in this tale of interracial marriage ending in wife-murder.[19] Is that curious pleasure or catharsis that tragedy is supposed to engender in its audience here the perverse, illiberal, atavistic pleasure of seeing an interracial marriage end in catastrophe and the spectacular downfall of a high-ranking black man? Charles Marowitz has his angry black separatist Iago turn to the audience in *An Othello*: 'I do declare, I ain't never know'd a black man shack up with a white woman

15

without it bringin' him heartache and misery.'[20] The play does little to challenge this racialised fatalism. Few critics have been willing to acknowledge what must surely be true: that the play is inevitably and inescapably racist and could not be otherwise. It speaks to, and out of, a racism that is deeply imbricated in its conception and reception.

It would be easier simply to identify racist beliefs with particular characters in the play. Racial unease, however, cannot simply be attributed to those who voice it explicitly, such as Iago, Roderigo or Brabanzio; nor can it be attributed to Shakespeare himself; rather, it is a function of the *play itself* to struggle with troubling concepts of marital and cultural union through a language that tugs persistently into disharmony and separateness. Laurie Maguire argues that 'the play approves Desdemona's choice of the black Othello as husband by showing us the inadequacies of the white Venetian alternatives'[21] – and I'll discuss the allure of this kind of reading for recent readers and critics in the next chapter – but the play's rhetorical mode seems to undercut even this apparent, and rather negative endorsement. Just because Roderigo is a dolt does not mean that the play has found all Venetian manhood deficient, and therefore we cannot adduce support for the marriage on these grounds alone. Indeed, one of the features of Shakespeare's dramatic compression of the story he found in Cinthio is the elision of a period of happy marriage before the move to Cyprus: 'they were united in marriage and lived together in such concord and tranquillity while they remained in Venice, that never a word passed between them that was not loving.'[22] Instead, Shakespeare gives us a liaison that is, from the outset, marked by social prohibition and structural disturbance. When Boswell and Johnson conversed about the play, Boswell 'observed the great defect of the tragedy of *Othello* was, that it had not a moral; for that no man could resist the circumstances of suspicion which were artfully suggested to Othello's mind'. Johnson disagreed, proposing that '*Othello* has more moral than almost any play', chief among which was 'this very useful moral, not to make an unequal match'.[23] While we are now less concerned with the morality of Shakespearian tragedy, Johnson's sense that the play does not fully endorse the love of Desdemona and Othello requires our attention.

16

Johnson's 'unequal' is, of course, a euphemism. The match is not 'unequal' primarily in terms of rank, wealth or interests – the primary concerns of eighteenth-century matrimonial decorum. Nor is it even 'unequal' primarily in terms of age, despite Othello's admission that he is 'declined/ Into the vale of years' (3.3.269–70). Rather, it is unequal in racial terms. Even – especially – when it is not explicit, race is a factor in responses to the play. Racism is 'institutional' in *Othello* – by which I mean that it is and has been a foundational tenet of its writing and its ongoing reception, an enabling condition of its creation and reproduction. It is not attributable specifically to any individual in the play or outside it, but rather to the institutional mechanisms of writing, reading and performance. Rather than identifying and reprimanding racism as a property of particular characters or critics, we need to acknowledge it as a complex part of the play's terrifying appeal, as the next chapter will detail. Here, I want to discuss how instances of duplication, repetition and disjunction serve as echoes of and displacements for the play's racial dynamic. Othello's marriage to Desdemona marks a fundamental trangression of boundaries – between black and white, male and female, military and domestic, self and other – and the play responds to and encodes this central breach in a number of formal, thematic and rhetorical instances of duplication, substitution and exchange.

Othello is a play that repeatedly avoids action, or, rather, substitutes words for action. Brabanzio's armed neighbours are thwarted in their attempt to seize Othello, who has already been called to the council. Iago's attempts to stir up trouble are initially forestalled by Othello's majestic 'Keep up your bright swords, for the dew will rust 'em' (1.2.60). The outraged father's protestations about the theft of his daughter lead the Duke to promise firm punishment from the 'bloody book of law' (1.3.67), but, when it is revealed that the valuable and respected general Othello is the thief, thoughts of penalty are dropped. The cause of this nocturnal commotion, the threat to Cyprus from the Turkish fleet, turns out to be 'a pageant/ – To keep us in false gaze' (1.3.19–20): the promised sea battle and the defence of Cyprus are also stepped down, just as concerns about Othello's safety in the stormy seas prove unnecessary when he lands without injury. In place of fighting the Turkish invaders in defence of Christendom itself, the play offers only the parodic and unedifying scuffle of an orchestrated drunken brawl. In repeatedly proposing scenes of active engagement and then dispersing them, the play could be seen to be structured anticlimactically. Rather, it internalizes these avoided actions so that the most distinctive stage moments are of psychological rather than physical interaction, and so that physical actions seem to externalize what is 'too hideous to be shown' (3.3.112) – the travails of the mind. Verdi's opera *Otello* abandons all of the play's Act 1, beginning dramatically with the storm, thereby suggesting that this is a metaphor for the social and psychic disturbances that have gone before, and that, more significantly, are to come. Thus Act 3 Scene 3, the pivot of the play, gives us an extraordinary and extended sequence of move and counter-move, of realization and counter-realization, as Iago brings Othello from the exquisite marital security of 'perdition catch my soul/ But I do love thee' (3.3.91–2) to 'damn her, lewd minx' (3.3.478) in the space of 400 lines. Something fundamental, something irreversible, has happened, but it is an inner, psychic shift rather than an external and physical one.

There is one significant exception to this pattern of psychological rather than physical action. The transmission of the fatal handkerchief, inherited and then gifted by Othello, dropped by Desdemona, picked up by Emilia, passed on to Iago, planted on Cassio and offered to Bianca, shows us the stage prop that binds the main players in the drama in an increasingly claustrophobic web, and that symbolizes the transmission of Iago's cankerous jealousy.

As Karen Newman has argued, the handkerchief seems to function as 'a snowballing signifier, for, as it passes from hand to hand, both literal and critical, it accumulates myriad associations and meanings'.[24] In its suggestion of both love and tears it encapsulates the movement of the play. Without it the tragedy could not occur as it does: Julie Hankey's stage history quotes the actor Margaret Webster, who, as Emilia, entered the stage during a rehearsal of Act 3 Scene 3 to find the handkerchief had been forgotten by the stage manager. The consequences flashed through her mind: 'no handkerchief, no play. I couldn't give it to Iago, he couldn't plant it on Cassio, Othello couldn't see Cassio give it to Bianca, Iago couldn't use that to prove Desdemona's guilt – the whole play fell to pieces like a house of cards'.[25] In addition to this material centrality to the plot, however, the handkerchief also gathers up a number of symbolic associations. The handkerchief is both entirely domestic and simultaneously exotic, associated with witchcraft and sorcery, as well as with the native English fruits strawberries. The embroidery has been seen by many critics to be emblematic of spots of blood, and thus metonymically related to the spotted wedding sheets and to the loss of virginity. Othello bestows it with different meanings when he discusses it in Act 3 and again in Act 5. Firstly he describes

> That handkerchief
> Did an Egyptian to my mother give.
> She was a charmer, and could almost read
> The thoughts of people. She told her, while she kept it
> 'Twould make her amiable, and subdue my father
> Entirely to her love; but if she lost it,
> Or made a gift of it, my father's eye
> Should hold her loathèd, and his spirits should hunt
> After new fancies. She, dying, gave it me
> And bid me, when my fate would have me wived,
> To give it her.
>
> (3.4.55–65)

He tells Desdemona 'there's magic in the web of it' (3.4.69), thus endowing the handkerchief with the sorcery he earlier denies using, and, indeed, the prediction that the loss of the handkerchief would mean the loss of love is borne out in the play. In Act 5, however, Othello talks about the sentimental significance of the handkerchief as a lover's gift across two generations rather than as an object with magical properties:

> that recognizance and pledge of love
> Which I first gave her. ...
> It was a handkerchief, an antique token
> My father gave my mother.
>
> (5.2.221–4).

What is important about the handkerchief as a symbol is its singularity, and yet it is strangely and repeatedly doubled. On finding the dropped handkerchief, Emilia determines to 'ha' the work ta'en out' – to have it copied. She will then 'give't Iago'

19

(3.3.300–1). It is not clear from the pronouns here whether she proposes to give her husband the original or the copy of the handkerchief. When Cassio offers Bianca the handkerchief he finds 'in [his] chamber' (3.4.185), he again asks her to 'take me this work out' (3.4.177): 'I like the work well. Ere it be demanded – /As like enough it will – I would have it copied' (3.4.186–7). It may be that this is the textual equivalent of what anatomists call a 'vestigial organ': the classic case is the human appendix, which is thought to have had an earlier physiological function that evolution has made redundant. In Cinthio's source, the corporal has the work copied by a woman 'who worked the most wonderful embroidery on lawn', and, to prove his allegations about Disdemona's infidelity, the Ensign brings the Moor to where he can see the woman working on the copy of the handkerchief by the light from the street window.[26] Shakespeare has changed the story so that it is by watching Cassio discuss Bianca but making Othello believe he is referring to Desdemona that Iago consolidates Othello's jealousy: the play thus has no place for the repeated idea of copying the handkerchief. But, in the context of the wider themes of doubleness and duplication, it is striking that, for the original donor and receiver of the handkerchief, it is irreplaceable, but the others who hold it are struck by the ease with which it can be copied. On the one hand, the strange 'wonder' (3.4.99) in the handkerchief is its uniqueness. Its distinctive strawberry embroidery means that it is instantly recognizable. Iago tells Othello he has seen Cassio wipe his beard with 'such a handkerchief/ –I am sure it was your wife's' (3.3.442–3), and the implicit sense that there could be no other similar handkerchief is crucial to the force of its placement in Cassio's chamber. On the other hand, its embroidery can be copied, duplicated, made over and over again. In this double sense, then, the handkerchief functions as the locus of anxieties about sexual fidelity and exclusivity in marriage: Douglas Bruster argues that 'in copying this pattern – or at least by implying that it *can* be copied – Emilia [as, we might add, does Cassio] articulates a rationale for Othello's anxiety: the fear that he can be replaced sexually'.[27]

The handkerchief thus serves as a metonym for sexual anxiety, and as the central example of a pattern of duplications and substitutions that inform the play. Othello's fear that he can be replaced sexually is central to Cassio's representation in Shakespeare's play. Michael Neill notes that Shakespeare makes the apparently insignificant but telling change to the source story: in place of Cinthio's rank of 'captain' or 'corporal' he makes Cassio 'lieutenant', a word he uses only rarely elsewhere in his plays but that is insistently stressed in over twenty occurrences in *Othello*. Neill argues that 'the word had not yet stabilized to its modern meaning and still carried a good deal of its original French sense, "one holding [another's] place".'[28] Cassio is thus Othello's professional replacement or substitute: his general's anxiety is that his lieutenant deputizes for him in the bedroom also. Of course, Cassio is a stalking-horse substitute in another sense – the real threat to Othello and Desdemona's marriage is not the Florentine ladies' man but the malevolent figure of Iago. The lieutenancy is a figure for a network of substitutes and duplications that haunt the play. As the plot unfolds, Iago assumes the role he had coveted from the outset: 'I know my price, I am worth no worse a place' (1.1.11). This moment of triumph is often marked in performance by his taking on the insignia of the lieutenancy stripped from the disgraced Cassio. Othello's 'now art thou my lieutenant' (3.3.481) substitutes Iago for Cassio even as Iago substitutes for Desdemona in the perverted marriage ceremony that is the male 'sacred vow' (3.3.464) of revenge: 'Witness you ever-burning lights above' (3.3.466). The stage business specified in the promptbook for Trevor Nunn's Royal Shakespeare Company production of 1989 makes this association with marriage stronger: 'Ot[hello] take I[ago's] hand. I[ago] kiss Ot[hello's] hand put his on top.'[29]

The play's abiding fear of adulterous exchange and interchange can be connected to its ambivalence about the capitalist culture of Venice that Othello, as the state's greatest general, is busy defending. Venice was a city-state rich from trade. The Renaissance significance of Cyprus, like that of Venice's other colonial outposts in the Mediterranean, was to hold a Venetian garrison to protect these lucrative trading and shipping routes. Exchange and commerce were dominant in early modern perceptions of Venice, functions it shared with another entrepreneurial metropolis dependent on sea trade, London itself. Related to this mercantile ethos was a strong association with prostitution, both literal and figurative, in the sense of a feminized city selling herself to passing ships. Thomas Coryat, who wrote about his visit to the city in 1611, noted that Venice was 'famoused over all Christendom' for courtesans, and illustrated this contention with a voluptuous naked-breasted example.[30] Thus, for early modern Londoners Venice functioned ambivalently as a civic exemplar at once positive and negative.

The association of Venice with sexual licence is a strong element of the play. The flip side of the commercialized sex of prostitution – the idealized maiden rather than the denigrated whore – is also economically constructed. In the opening scene, Iago alerts Brabanzio to 'thieves, thieves, thieves' (1.1.79) and tells him 'you're robbed' (86); when Brabanzio catches up with Othello, he hails him 'foul thief' (1.2.63); and in the Council he describes Desdemona as 'stol'n from me' (1.3.60). Iago describes Othello's marriage as a valuable act of piracy: 'he tonight hath boarded a land-carrack./ If it prove lawful prize, he's made for ever' (1.2.50–1), and later vows to undo Desdemona's 'credit' with her husband (2.3.350). Brabanzio's ironic dismissal of his daughter as 'jewel' (1.3.194) and the Duke's aphoristic advice 'the robbed that smiles steals something from the thief' (1.3.207) all partake of a shared discourse of women as property. As Neill notes, 'women are to men rather as Cyprus is to Venice and Turkey – objects of competition, possession and "occupation"'.[31] The idea that Venetian women are loose is a stereotype Iago invokes to ensnare Othello, who accuses his wife: 'I took you for that cunning whore of Venice/ That married with Othello' (4.2.93–4).

A romantic reading of the play would hope that the unorthodox relationship of Othello and Desdemona might break through this language of sexual possession and denigration. However, the idea of love as economic property and possession is not merely a Venetian habit of thought, or, at least, it is an aspect of the host community that Othello has enthusiastically adopted. Even at his most romantic, as the couple prepare to withdraw and leave the islanders and soldiers to their festivities, Othello's language is tainted with the mercenary:

> Come, my dear love,
> The purchase made, the fruits are to ensue.
> The profit's yet to come 'tween me and you.
>
> (2.3.8–10)

His increasing mental agony is thus inevitably expressed in terms of possession:

> O curse of marriage,
> That we can call these delicate creatures ours
> And not their appetites!
>
> (3.3.272–4)

Even his realization of what he has done is cast in terms of monetary value: his final speech sees him occupy various positions of alterity including that of 'the base Indian [who] threw a pearl away/ Richer than all his tribe' (5.2.356–7). This Venetian imagery of value as commercially maintained rather than intrinsic infiltrates the language of exchange in the play: all is dangerously interchangeable, all can be bought, as Emilia notes when she asks 'who would not make her husband a cuckold to make him a monarch?' (4.3.74–5).

One exchange or equivalence that the play repeatedly suggests is between the relationship of Desdemona and Othello, and the threat by the Turks to Venetian interests. This equivalence is first suggested through structural juxtaposition. In the second scene of the play, two groups of men with lights converge on Othello's lodgings in quick succession. At the arrival of the first, Iago assumes that these are 'the raisèd father and his friends' (1.2.29) – the adjective 'raisèd' neatly evades the question of agency: how and by whom? In fact they are the messengers of the senate, requiring Othello's 'haste-post-haste appearance' (1.2.37), as news of the Turkish fleet has arrived in Venice. The personal is overridden by the political, but their simultaneity suggests the metaphorical connection between them. Brabanzio also feels certain that his complaint will be heard by the council, because, implicitly, the right of a father is central to civic justice:

> The Duke himself,
> Or any of my brothers of the state,
> Cannot but feel this wrong as 'twere their own;

For if such actions may have passage free,
Bondslaves and pagans shall our statesmen be.

(1.2.96–100)

The word 'pagan' links the 'theft' of Desdemona, and Othello himself, to the Turkish threat: if this behaviour is allowed in Venice we may as well be ruled by the Turk, such is Brabanzio's equation of private and public threat.

The Duke's attempts to comfort Brabanzio on the loss of his daughter make this clear: his end-stopped rhymes, which Brabanzio mockingly echoes, seem to indicate the cheerlessness of his sententious advice:

What cannot be preserved when fortune takes,
Patience her injury a mockery makes.
The robbed that smiles steals something from the thief;
He robs himself that spends a bootless grief.
BRABANZIO. So let the Turk of Cyprus us beguile,
We lose it not so long as we can smile.

(1.3.205–10)

Brabanzio's explicit equivalence here between the loss of his daughter and the threat to Cyprus activates a dualism always implicit in the play's representation of Othello, as both threat to order and preserver of it. As Jonathan Bate observes, the echo between 'Othello' and 'Ottoman' in the Duke's commission – 'Valiant Othello, we must straight employ you/Against the general enemy Ottoman' (1.3.48–9) – would be strengthened by the apparent pronunciation of the eponymous hero's name as 'Otello'.[32] We might also observe at this point the curious slippage of 'general', a word used twenty-six times in the play to refer to Othello, which is here attached to the Turkish enemy. In the familial context Othello stands for the marauding Turk; in the civic context he leads the fleet against that Turk. Here in Venice the two aspects are in potential conflict, but both come together again in the delivered speech of the herald in Cyprus in Act 2 Scene 2. Othello has announced a dual celebration of the news of the 'mere perdition of the Turkish fleet' (2.2.3) and 'his nuptial' (2.2.7): here there seems no difficulty in the juxtaposition. For a moment, the play hangs in a happy stasis: both the marriage and the battle are successfully concluded.

However, the threat that Venetians may 'turn Turk' – that Othello's double status as threat and defence might spread – is one of the play's most pressing and slippery dualisms. Whereas the external, actual threat from the Turkish fleet is quickly neutralized by a fortuitous storm, the real threat to the world of the play comes from an internalized foe, the Turk within. This concept first emerges casually. Iago uses the phrase: 'it is true, or else I am a Turk' (2.1.117), justifying his jovial remarks to Desdemona and Emilia as they wait anxiously on the quayside for news of Othello. Here it functions as an impossibility: how could Iago be a Turk? therefore his words must be true, although the context makes this mocking rather than serious. Before long, however, the slippage between Venetian and Turk makes such assertions much more problematic. When Othello is roused from his bed by the carousing soldiers, his reprimand is firm:

> Are we turned Turks, and to ourselves do that
> Which heaven hath forbid the Ottomites?
> For Christian shame, put by this barbarous brawl.

> (2.3.163–5)

Iago's response slyly equates the brawlers with 'bride and groom/ Devesting them for bed' (2.3.173–4), further interconnecting the disturbance with the marriage. Othello's implication is clear: the soldiers have become the threat, the enemy within, now that the spectre of an external foe has disappeared. Iago's cry 'mutiny' (2.3.150) is expressive of the sense of threat the cooped-up soldiers, starved of real conflict and on high alert in the Cypriot outpost, pose to the civil order. Kenneth Tynan, writing of John Dexter's 1964 production, noted that here the fight developed into 'a popular riot, with the mutinous Cypriots rising against their Venetian overlords. Thus Othello has something more to quell than a private quarrel'.[33]

The opposition between Venetian and Turk, between the Christian and the barbarous, is a dualism that recurs again and again throughout the play, and that has its most striking expression in Othello's own speech before his suicide. Like other of Shakespeare's tragic heroes, Othello's final concern is for his reputation and for the transmission of his story. He instructs the onlookers in his own version of what has

happened, denying that he was 'easily jealous', claiming instead
that he is 'one that loved not wisely but too well' (5.2.353–4):

> And say besides that in Aleppo once,
> Where a malignant and a turbaned Turk
> Beat a Venetian and traduced the state,
> I took by th'throat the circumcisèd dog
> And smote him thus.
>
> *He stabs himself.*
>
> (5.2.361–5)

The complex forms of alienation and identification knitted up in
this speech make it a terrifying condensation of the destructive
power of that running oxymoron 'The Moor of Venice'. Othello
seems to be back in story-telling mode, the form in which he
wooed and won Desdemona, but here his genre is tragedy
rather than romantic comedy. The Turkish port of Aleppo is the
scene for a miniature racial psychodrama that has to end in
Othello's death at his own hand. As the logic of his anecdote
makes clear, he is both the 'malignant and ... turbaned Turk'
who speaks ill of Venice and must therefore be smote 'thus', and
the hand doing the smiting, the defender of the reputation of
Venice and of its citizen. Othello seems to recognize himself
both as the threat to the Venetian state and as its only true
defender, and to figure his suicide not as private remorse for the
murder of his beloved and innocent wife but as public
atonement for, and fatal reconciliation of, his dangerously
anomalous position in the state. It is a complicated representation of the forces of belonging and alienation that simultaneously bind Othello to the state and repel him from it. Those
two meanings of 'of', signalling belonging and separation, are
violently ruptured. And, crucially, the speech makes a final and
fatal implicit connection between the transgressive marriage of
Othello and Desdemona, and the civic order of Venice itself.
Desdemona can therefore function symbolically as a representation of Venice – the feminized city accused of whoredom – as
their marriage plays out a scaled-down geo-political conflict in
which Moor and Turk are equivalent and insidious threats to the
city-state. At the last reckoning it is Venice Othello has
damaged, not simply his private marriage. The Venetians come
to Cyprus to take over his command, but he outwits them, even
as he does their work for them. (Marowitz's Iago tells Othello

'when you turn that blade onto yourself, you're doin' whitey's work. You just fallin' into his set-up.'[34]) In Parker's film, Cassio, in a last act of devoted friendship, slips Othello the knife that enables him to die as a Venetian, taking his own revenge. Even death cannot, however, suture the split psyche of Othello, the Moor of Venice: rather, death gives him the opportunity to theatricalize that self-division, that doubleness, that oxymoron he fatally embodies.

2

Race and *Othello*

Why does Othello, in that final speech, shift the question of racial otherness into the multifarious exoticism of Aleppo, the 'turbaned Turk', 'Arabian trees', 'base Indian' (5.2.356–62) – or, as some texts modernize the Folio's 'Iudean', 'Judean' – all the while ignoring the identity of 'Moor' with which the play labels him from its title onwards? Shifting ideas of racial difference are a crucial – and problematic – aspect of the play and of its reception. When American literature professor Emily Bartels notes that her students, on reading *Othello*, always want to talk about race, she implies that this 'so often tend[s] to simplify the story'.[1] Rather it seems to me to complicate it in ways that force us to acknowledge similarities and differences between our own perspectives and those of early modern audiences, which bring us up against notions of prejudice that cannot be comfortably consigned to history, and that implicate us in the racially configured discourses out of which the play was written and in which it has continued to be read and performed. Far from simplifying *Othello* and Othello, questions of race engage us in complex narratives of belonging and alienation. *Othello* has shaped racial understanding in a range of ways unthinkable to Shakespeare and his original audiences: as the novelist Ben Okri has observed, if it 'is not a play about race, then its history has made it one'.[2] Martin Wine laments the way in which 'modernity, alas, thrusts itself willy-nilly upon the play'; Julie Hankey describes the 'patina of *apparent* topicality' the play has acquired.[3] These, too, seem to underestimate the subtlety, the inevitability and the challenge of these forms of topicality, as perhaps the dominant claim *Othello* has on our twenty-first-century attention. When Janet Suzman produced the play in the Market Theatre of Johannesburg during apartheid, she and John Kani, who played Othello, were '*at last*', fired up after ten frustrating years of keeping a constant vigil for the play that might speak not just to both of us as actors but to our anguished country'; when the African-American actor Paul Robeson took on the role, he observed that Othello 'in the Venice of that time was in practically the same position as a coloured man in America today':[4] both comments attest to the ongoing fact of the play's unsettling relevance.

It is too easy to assume that we can distance *Othello* from our own times and our own prejudices through careful and impeccably scholarly reconstructions of early seventeenth-century attitudes to black characters, when in fact our very categories of investigation may themselves be racially inflected. Perhaps it is even more dangerous to assume that we *should* attempt to separate our own racial blind spots and biases from those of the play. When, for example, scholars agonize over whether Shakespeare intended Othello as a tawny North African Arab – the literal associations of 'Moor' (first used at 1.1.39) and 'Barbary' (1.1.113) – or a black sub-Saharan African – Roderigo's slur 'thicklips' (1.1.66) – we may be justified in feeling that this is more a question about our own categories of racial difference than about those of the early Jacobean period. This sense of anachronism is heightened by the corollary of these arguments about Othello's provenance, which tends to suggest that the lighter his complexion, the more noble and tragic the character. Thus that *Othello* has always been about race is certain; that it has always been about the racial assumptions of its readers and audience members needs to be analysed as part of its ongoing tradition; that we cannot step outside its, and our, assumptions interpolates us as coadjutants in its compelling, terrifying mixture of racial fantasy.

We have only one possible illustration of a Shakespeare play in contemporary performance. It is not of *Othello* but it may be able to help us identify something of that play's first emotional charge for audiences who saw it at the Globe in 1603–4. The illustration, known as the Peacham drawing, apparently depicts a scene from the early tragedy *Titus Andronicus*, in which Tamora, captive Queen of the Goths, pleads for the life of her sons before the Roman general Titus (Fig. 2). Titus, the main character of the drama, occupies the middle of the picture bearing a staff: the sight lines seem to focus in on him. The composition of the tableau is, however, dominated and

Figure 2. 'Peacham' drawing of *Titus Andronicus*.

decentred by a figure on the far right. He is the black Moor Aaron, his colour represented in the drawing not by cross-hatching or shading but by solid dark ink. Otherness, difference, is the defining characteristic of his depiction, rendered non-naturalistic in its blank density. The dominant message the picture conveys about the play on the stage is the visual force of Aaron's blackness and his control over the composition. The Peacham drawing thus gives us an unexpected visual analogue for the themes of *Titus Andronicus* itself: while Titus and Tamora take centre stage, Aaron's oblique and insistent presence on the sidelines dominates the play. It is he who, in a first soliloquy worthy of one of Christopher Marlowe's overreaching hero characters such as Tamburlaine, who held sway on the London stage of the early 1590s, vows 'Away with slavish weeds and servile thoughts!' (2.1.18); he encourages the sons of his lover Tamora to rape Lavinia because 'vengeance is in my heart, death in my hand,/ Blood and revenge are hammering in my head' (2.3.38-9); he plants treasure to frame the sons of Titus; and he persuades Titus to chop off his hand in a trick bargain to free his already-murdered sons. Finally, he resolutely refuses the traditional gesture of repentance in the face of death, regretting only 'that I had not done ten thousand more' wicked deeds (5.1.124). This early prominence of a black character, both structurally and visually, may have made it inevitable that Shakespeare would return to the theme.

So what would audiences have made of a black hero? One important way to discuss this theme is historically, or, as Arthur Little puts it, 'Shakespeare's pre-text, what the audience knows before it comes to experience the play'.[5] Much of this pre-text, as discussed below, comes from cultural assumptions rather than from direct contact with actual black people, but there are two main challenges to this assumption. That black people were perceived as sufficiently numerous in late sixteenth century England to be a threat is attested by a series of communiqués from the Queen on the matter of repatriation – although the history of racism tells us that anxious perceptions of the number of immigrants frequently grossly exceed actual demography. In 1596, in an open letter to the Lord Mayor and Aldermen of London, from Queen Elizabeth, we read:

Her Majesty understanding that there are of late divers blackmoors brought into this realm, of which kind of people there are already here too many, considering how God hath blessed this land with great increase of people of our own nation as any country in the world, whereof many for want of service and means to set them on work fall to idleness and to great extremity. Her Majesty's pleasure therefore is that those kind of people should be sent forth of this land, and for that purpose there is direction given to this bearer Edward Banes to take of those blackmoors that in this last voyage under Sir Thomas Baskervile were brought into this realm the number of ten, to be transported by him out of the realm.

In the same year Captain Caspar van Senden's request for a licence to deport 'blackmoors ... into Spain and Portugal' was approved:

Her Majesty ... considereth ... that those kind of people may be well spared in this realm, being so populous and numbers of able persons the subjects of the land and Christian people that perish for want of service, whereby through their labour they might be maintained. [You] are therefore required ... to aid and assist him to take up such blackmoors as he shall find within this realm, with the consent of their masters, who we doubt not, considering her Majesty's good pleasure to have those kind of people sent out of the land ... and that they shall do charitably and like Christians rather to be served by their own countrymen than with those kind of people, will yield those in their possession to him.[6]

This licence was renewed five years later in 1601.

These documents identify black people as servants or slaves – 'those in their possession' – but the second piece of relevant evidence associates Moors with nobility. The arrival of a courtly delegation from Barbary in North Africa in late 1600 caused a considerable stir in London. Led by the Moroccan ambassador Abdul El-Quahéd Ben Messasud, the emissaries were in England for six months, during which time Shakespeare's company, the Lord Chamberlain's Men, performed at court. An extant portrait (Fig. 3) of the ambassador shows an imperious figure wearing a pale turban, with a dark moustache and short beard, a hooked nose and a direct and piercing stare. His light-coloured garments are covered with a dark cloak and he wears an ornate sword. Looking at the portrait, Ernst Honigmann asks: 'Is it too fanciful to suppose that this very face haunted

Figure 3. Abdul El-Quahéd Ben Messasud,
Moorish Ambassador to Queen Elizabeth I.

33

Shakespeare's imagination and inspired the writing of his tragedy?[7] It *is* certainly fanciful, but there is no doubt that the idea of Barbary reverberates throughout the play's verbal texture. Othello is called 'Barbary horse' (1.1.113–14) and 'erring barbarian' (1.3.354), and the word and some unexpected cognates recur visually and acoustically through the play, from Brabanzio, called Barbantio at several points in the stage directions and speech prefixes, the 'barbarous' brawl of 2.3.165, to the melancholy story of the maid called Barbary in 4.3.25–32.

Shakespeare inherited a black hero from the nameless Moor who is one of Cinthio's central protagonists. It is hard to see what specific value, if any, attaches itself to the ethnicity of the Moor in the source. Critics sometimes assert that Cinthio's is a didactic story in which the racially mixed marriage is presented as a negative exemplar, but, although his Disdemona, observing her jealous husband's unwarranted coolness towards her, fears she will 'be a warning to young girls not to marry against their parents' wishes; and Italian ladies will learn by my example not to tie themselves to a man whom Nature, Heaven, and manner of life separate from us',[8] Cinthio's narrator does not actually push the point home in his commentary. Here, the socio-moral connotations of the Moor's race are not made explicit, and Cinthio's story stresses the extent to which his central protagonist is valued by the Venetian state. Audiences at the play's first performances, however, would have brought a host of associations, derived from a nexus of textual and material experiences, to the idea of a black character. Blackness was frequently associated with the devil and with wickedness: Reginald Scot, in his *The Discovery of Witchcraft* (1584), opined that 'a damned soul may and doth take the shape of a black moor' and in Samuel Harsnett's *A Declaration of Egregious Popish Impostures* (1603), known to have been read by Shakespeare, since he draws on it for names of devils in *King Lear*, a woman is tempted by a demon in the shape of 'a black man standing at the door and beckoning her to come away'. Thomas Heywood, in a play about travelling and English imperialism called *The Fair Maid of the West II* (1630), described 'a Moor/ Of all that bears man's shape likest a devil'.[9] Emilia refers to this same tradition when she calls Othello 'the blacker devil' after the discovery of the murder of Desdemona, 'the more angel she' (5.2.140). Black characters on stage before *Othello* tended therefore to be villains, often clever, plotting and amoral, rather like *Titus Andronicus*'s Aaron. In George Peele's *The Battle of Alcazar* (1598), the bombastic soldier Muly Hamet is described as 'black in his look, and bloody in his deeds', although he is flanked by an opposite 'brave barbarian lord Muly Molocco'.[10] In (?) Thomas Dekker's *Lust's Dominion* (1600), Eleazar is a black character combining sexual transgression and machiavellian plotting. Even in a comedy, sexual predation of white women is seen as defining black masculinity. In a comic prototype for Othello's courtship of Desdemona, another Venetian play sees another woman whose marriage choices are again controlled by a father. All suitors for Portia in *The Merchant of Venice* must undertake a choice between metallic caskets, and the Prince of Morocco's bad choice of the gold casket means that he is unsuccessful. As he leaves, Portia remarks 'let all of his complexion choose me so' (2.7.79). As Virginia Mason Vaughan summarizes, in plays before *Othello*, including those by Shakespeare, 'black skin signalled, in addition to visual ugliness, an ingrained moral infection, a taint in the blood often linked to sexual perversion and the desire to possess a white woman'.[11]

Many of the expectations evoked by the spectacle of a black character, therefore, were part of a long cultural tradition. This tradition was scarcely modified by the travellers' tales and exploration narratives that filled London's booksellers during the second half of the sixteenth century and beyond. George Best's account of the scriptural basis for different skin colours was published as part of Richard Hakluyt's monumental *The Principal Navigations Voyages Traffiques and Discoveries of the English Nation* (published in three volumes between 1598 and 1600), in which he attributed blackness to the sin of Cham in defying God's prohibition on sexual intercourse in the ark:

> for the which wicked and detestable fact, as an example for contempt of Almighty God, and disobedience of parents, God would a son should be born whose name was Chus, who not only itself, but all his posterity after him should be so black and loathsome, that it might remain a spectacle of disobedience to all the world. And of this black and cursed Chus came all these black Moors which are in Africa.[12]

Sexual depravity and prowess were frequently associated with blackness in travel narratives, an association Roderigo articulates when he dubs Othello 'a lascivious Moor' (1.1.128). Leo Africanus, himself a converted Moor living in Italy, maintained that 'Negroes' 'have great swarms of harlots among them; whereupon a man may easily conjecture their manner of living' and that no people were 'more prone to venery' than the North African; other travellers discussed African tribes 'which like beasts live without wedding and dwell with women without law'.[13] Surveying these narratives, Karen Newman concludes that 'always we find the link between blackness and the monstrous, and particularly a monstrous sexuality'; and Arthur Little concurs that *Othello* is working with and against existing stereotypes as a 'text that will at once unsettle and fill in, substantiate and resolve what the audience suspects it already knows about the essence of blackness as the savage and libidinous Other'.[14]

Black characters were, therefore, already associated with stereotypical lust for sex and power. It could be argued that Shakespeare challenges these assumptions in *Othello*. Here he apparently splits the conventional black role – exemplified by Muly Hamet, Aaron and Eleazar – into two, allocating its Machiavellian malignity to Iago, and its skin colour and sexuality to Othello. Many of the stereotypical attributes of blackness are thus identified with Iago: a man whose concept of sex is entirely physical; a plotter bent on revenge; the 'devil' (5.2.293) who cannot be killed at the end of the play. Whether or not Iago is explicitly racially motivated is difficult to judge, although his injunction to Cassio to drink 'the health of black Othello' (2.3.28–9) has more than a smack of racism. Perhaps it is rather that he fixes on the weakness of others, and sees that Othello's outsider status is a point of vulnerability. In the 1989 Royal Shakespeare Company production directed by Trevor Nunn, it was Iago's own sense of being a class outsider, an 'other rank' among the high-born officer class, that was more evident than his sense of Othello as an outsider, and the idea of a clever and embittered proletarian Iago has been a strong tradition in performance. However, it is part of the terrifying effectiveness of his psychological campaign that he focuses on the racial disparity between Othello and his new bride:

Not to affect many proposèd matches
Of her own clime, complexion, and degree,
Whereto we see in all things nature tends.
Foh, one may smell in such a will most rank,
Foul disproportions, thoughts unnatural!

(3.3.234-8)

Laurie Maguire notes that the associations of Iago's name foreground the racial *agon* of his complex relation to Othello:

Moor hater or Moor conqueror. Santiago (Saint Iago or St James) is the military patron of Spain. One of his most famous exploits occurred in 939 CE when he helped King Ramirez deliver Castile from the Moors, killing 60,000 Moors in battle. Consequently 'Santiago' became the war-cry of the Spanish armies, and Santiago is traditionally depicted on a white charger trampling the Moors underfoot. Every time the name 'Iago' drops with helpless unconsciousness from the Moor's lips, Shakespeare's audience remembered what we have long forgotten: that Santiago's great role in Spain was as enemy to the invading Moor, who was figurehead there of the Muslim kingdom.[15]

Historic Christian victories over Islam were particularly current in the London of 1603–4, the period of the play's composition. Richard Knollys's *The Generall Historie of the Turkes* (1603) was dedicated to the new king, James I, in recognition of the sovereign's own poem on the victory at Lepanto, which was promptly reprinted in England on his accession to the throne. James described Lepanto, in terms echoed by *Othello*, as an epic battle 'Betwixt the baptiz'd race,/ And circumsised Turband Turkes'.[16]

It may be that recent criticism's particular focus on the play's racial dynamic has obscured the importance of religion to the early modern category of 'Moor'. A dominant meaning of 'Moor' was 'Muslim', and a new consciousness of a twenty-first-century conflict, where 'the battle-lines reinflect those of the sixteenth-century Mediterranean, waging the forces of global capitalism against the imperatives of Islamic fundamentalism',[17] has brought another relevance to the play. But here Othello is again paradoxical, a divided or in-between figure. When Iago discusses previous campaigns 'at Rhodes, at Cyprus, and on other grounds/ Christened and heathen' (1.1.28–9), he identifies Othello on the side of the Christians. Many productions have assumed that the Othello who bids Desdemona pray before her murder and who swears 'by heaven' more frequently than all the other characters in the play put together is a convert to Christianity, and that when Iago vows to make him 'renounce his baptism' (2.3.334) he is referring to this conversion. In Olivier's interpretation of the role, the process of Othello's downfall was seen as an anti- or de-conversion, marked when, at 3.3.463, 'yon marble heaven', with 'a surging atavistic roar – he tears the crucifix from his neck and flings it into the air. Othello's a Moor again'.[18] In taking on what Bate calls 'the insignia of Islam' – the Turk's turban and circumcision he acknowledges in his final speeches – Othello might be seen to reject Christianity and die a Muslim, but this pattern of conversion and reversion exemplifies the motif of binary slippage that the play elaborates.[19]

In fact, the motif of slippage, or the board game's reliance on turning those double-sided counters back and forth, makes interpretative clarity about the play's articulation of racial and religious alterity difficult to achieve. Those characters in the play who articulate explicitly racist sentiments – Iago, Roderigo, Brabanzio – are not ones whose opinions or behaviour the play otherwise endorses, and it is surely significant that at no point in his relationship with Othello does the wronged Cassio ever play the race card. In more recent times, the play has not been entirely susceptible to a racially politicized reading: when Charles Marowitz wanted the play to coincide with contemporary black power discourses in 1972 he had to rewrite it as *An Othello*, in which Iago and Othello are both black – Othello as an Uncle Tom figure seeking assimilation and acceptance, Iago as an angry, politicized Black Panther despising the black general for marrying 'Snow White. Cinderella. Marilyn Monroe. Miss World'. It is, as the preface tells us, the very 'unsubtlety of racism' that drives Marowitz's reworking. His Iago tells Othello that his sexual relationship with Desdemona is an unacknowledged microcosm of the burden of racialized history, a public, rather than a private, encounter: 'Did you tell her that everytime she moaned and cried and wriggled beneath you, it was music to your ears cause in your heart you were beatin' her, whippin' her, destroyin' her for her whiteness to atone for your blackness – for what her whiteness has done to your blackness'.[20]

38

Shakespeare presents Othello himself as noble, eloquent, well respected by the state, denying rather than flaunting sexuality:

> I therefor beg it not
> To please the palate of my appetite,
> Nor to comply with heat – the young affects
> In me defunct –

(1.3.261–4)

Desdemona's 'I saw Othello's visage in his mind' (1.3.252) suggests that her decision is in spite of his colour rather than because of it, although Robert Burton's *Anatomy of Melancholy* discusses, in his chapter on causes of love-melancholy, that 'a black man is a pearl in a fair woman's eye'.[21] Laurence Olivier discussed the play's particular eroticism: 'it's tremendously, highly sexual because it's a black man', and this clearly has as much to tell us about the context of his interpretation as of the play itself.[22] Arguably, Shakespeare seems to have turned the tables on racist expectations by showing us a black and a white character who have reversed the usual colour associations, performing the chromatic flip characteristic of the board game 'Othello'. Instead of the Moor as villain we have the Moor as hero.

There is a lot of truth in this vision of a play that challenges racial prejudices rather than endorsing them. Martin Orkin has argued that 'Shakespeare seems concerned to separate his hero from the fiction that the racist associations attached to his color allege', and that 'in its fine scrutiny of the mechanisms underlying Iago's use of racism, and in its rejection of human pigmentation as a means of identifying worth, the play, as it always has done, continues to oppose racism'.[23] Thus the play is about racism and its effects; rather than being itself racist, it pursues an actively anti-racist agenda. This is an attractive view. We have so much invested in the idea of Shakespeare as a repository for liberal humanist values that it is disquieting to have to acknowledge that, on occasion, his plays fail to buttress contemporary tolerant opinion. Similar critical ingenuity has been expended on *The Taming of the Shrew*, a play about troubling gender politics, and *The Merchant of Venice*, about troubling racial politics, in order to establish that they interrogate stereotypes and prejudicial attitudes rather than sanctioning them.

39

This approach can certainly work for *Othello* too. It is noteworthy, for example, that Othello's acceptance in Venice goes without explanation: no one in the play sees a need to account for his high position. This is in interesting contrast to a modernized version of the play made for British television in 2002. Andrew Davies's *Othello* gave us a black policeman, John Othello, whose career is flourishing despite some entrenched racist attitudes among senior officers. When race riots break out and the failure of community policing comes under the spotlight, Othello is promoted, leaping over several ranks to become chief of the police force at a time when a black face is needed as a symbol of a new commitment to diversity in policing. It is clear that this is a political appointment, and Othello's personal and professional catastrophe comes as no surprise to a racist establishment that appoints 'Jago' as his successor. It is as if the television version is so surprised that a black man could ever reach such a position that it has to explain it away.[24]

The play's own silence on this matter is therefore revealing. Othello is secure in the regard in which the Duke and the Council hold him: 'My services which I have done the signiory,/ Shall out-tongue his complaints' (1.2.18–19). Even at the very end of the play he is still drawing some satisfaction from his public position: 'I have done the state some service, and they know't (5.2.348). Indeed, it is clear that, while there is an external enemy to be faced, Othello is accepted and valorized by the Venetian authorities. Orson Welles's film shows a signal difference in the councillors' attitude in 1.3 to the entry of Brabanzio and that of Othello: only when the Moor enters do all, including the Duke, rise in respect. When he is summoned before the Council, he is greeted 'Valiant Othello' (1.3.48), and the Duke's willingness to punish even 'our proper son' (1.3.69) for the scandal of Desdemona's elopement falters immediately when the charge is laid at Othello's door. The Duke urges Brabanzio to 'take up this mangled matter at the best' (1.3.172), and tells him 'your son-in-law is far more fair than black' (1.3.290), punning on the moral associations of blackness. Othello's transgression is to leave the military sphere where he is a respected general and to attempt to move into the private. Brabanzio, according to his son-in-law, 'loved me, oft invited me,/ Still questioned me the story of my life' (1.3.127–8);

it is not that Othello is entirely rejected by this Venetian patron, more that there are social boundaries he should not attempt to cross. In Marowitz's *An Othello*, Brabantio asks the audience 'Would you like your daughter to marry one?'[25] He clearly anticipates audience support for his position: this may not be misguided. A BBC survey on attitudes to race in Britain conducted in 2002 revealed that over half those questioned would not be entirely happy if their child entered a relationship with someone of a different racial background.[26] Marowitz's Iago tells us it is only while Othello is militarily useful that he is suffered by the Venetian establishment, who 'ain't got too much use for black-bucks once the smoke clears ... let's face it, man, if'n we don't use 'em for cannon-fodder, what the hell we *goin'a* do with 'em.'[27] The suggestion is that this Othello has been blind to his real position in Venetian society.

At the start of Shakespeare's play, therefore, when Othello's role in the state is clearly shaped by the pressure of external foes and while his transgressive marriage is subsumed by matters of state, the play appears to challenge every aspect of the traditional depiction of black characters on the stage and in early modern culture. Othello himself is neither hungry for power for himself, nor portrayed as sexually voracious. But it is part of *Othello*'s continuing power to disturb us that, as events unfold, it may be that the stereotype, apparently bucked at the outset, turns out to have a terrible and enduring hold on Othello's power to act.

The play's double title, discussed in Chapter 1, articulates both the specificity of tragic individuality – 'the tragedy of Othello' – and the generality of the stereotype – 'the Moor of Venice' – and the interplay between individual and type is an intricate part of the play's dynamic. It seems that early references to the play tend to call it 'the Moor of Venice', as Barbara Everett observes when she notes the difference in kind in the funeral elegy for the actor Richard Burbage when his most famous roles are listed with the proper names 'young Hamlet', 'kind Lear', Hieronimo from Kyd's *The Spanish Tragedy*, and then the typecast 'grieved Moor'.[28] Iago, Roderigo, Brabanzio, Cassio, Montano, Lodovico, and even Desdemona each call Othello 'Moor', both in and out of his presence, although Othello never refers to himself in this way. The first printed text of the play also evokes the type rather than the individual at a significant point. When Iago's treachery is revealed by Emilia in the 1622 quarto, the stage direction states 'the Moore runnes at Iago'. It is the only time Othello is not given his proper name, as if at this, his lowest point, he has forfeited his specific personal identity under the pressure of the vengeful racial stereotype. Again, in the 'Names of the Actors' appended to the Folio text, Othello's designation as 'moore' is curiously asymmetric in relation to explanatory tags appended to other of the characters: Cassio as 'an honourable Lieutenant', Roderigo as 'a gull'd gentleman' and Iago as 'a Villaine'. Does the label 'moore' have the same explanatory clarity as the other descriptors? Throughout the play, the use of his proper name, Othello, is much less frequent than the designation 'Moor', and appears more often in the first half of the play than in the second. Interestingly, as Othello's jealousy mounts, he begins to refer to himself in the third person, as if he is alienated from his proper self: 'Othello's occupation's gone' (3.3.362); 'I took you for that cunning whore of Venice/ That married with Othello' (4.2.93–4); 'Where should Othello go?' (5.2.278). Most strikingly, his self-division is enacted syntactically when he responds to Lodovico's 'where is this rash and most unfortunate man?' with 'That's he that was Othello: here I am' (5.2.289–90): the I and 'Othello' have become irreparably split as chaos has come again.

It does seem that Othello begins to internalize the prevailing dynamic of Venetian society that denigrates blackness. Images of dirtying are a subtle reinforcement of white supremacy: in an unexpectedly colloquial phrase the Duke tells Othello he must 'slubber the gloss of your new fortunes' (1.3.225–6); Othello's altered behaviour is alluded to anxiously by Desdemona as if something 'hath puddled his clear spirit' (3.4.141); Iago vows that he will 'turn her virtue into pitch' (2.3.351); and Othello himself conceptualizes his changed view of his wife as a literal blackening:

> Her name, that was as fresh
> As Dian's visage, is now begrimed and black
> As mine own face.
>
> (3.3.391–3)

This is a reading from Q2, adopted by many editors, in preference to F's '*My* name': although the Folio reading is taken up by Welles's film, which shows us Othello looking into a mirror at this point, seeing himself as if for the first time in the way that others see him, or that Iago persuades him others see him. Here Othello's explicit comparison between the assumed fallen and besmirched adulterous wife and his own complexion, as in Q2, or his association of his skin colour with dirt, may attest to the self-loathing engendered by a racist society. James Agate wrote of African-American Paul Robeson's performance in 1930 that 'his whole bearing, gait, and diction were full of humility and apology: the inferiority complex in a word'.[29] When another black American Othello, James Earl Jones, put Desdemona's white hand in his on the line 'It is the cause' (5.2.1), he seemed to be acceding to some kind of inevitability about the outcome of the interracial marriage: the *New Yorker* reviewer felt that this interpretation 'opportunistically distorts and diminishes this resounding line into a comment on race prejudice'.[30] Repeated ideas of dirtying through these images also show a subconscious fear of contamination – the fear that the white will be blackened through contact with Othello. The idea that Othello may blacken – morally and racially – those around him is a prevalent one, and this symbolic point is often alluded to in a comically literal way. Almost every account of a production in which the Othello actor indicates his race through black make-up has an anecdote about this blackness coming off on other characters. Ellen Terry, for instance, complained that Henry Irving left her 'as black as he', and a famous 'dirty still' from John Dexter's 1964 production shows Maggie Smith as Desdemona smudged by Olivier's black make-up.[31] This is not only a recent anxiety: when the Spanish ambassador danced with a blacked-up Queen Anne in Jonson's *The Masque of Blackness* in 1605, his gallantry was observed when he 'forgot not to kiss her hand, though there was danger it would have left a mark on his lips'.[32]

Numerous critics have understood Othello's descent into an incoherent rage, marked by the degeneration of his speech into the exotic lubricity of 'goats and monkeys' (4.1.265), as a reversion to some kind of buried savagery. The speed of his conversion to Iago's poison, his public renunciation of his wife, and the peculiarly ritualistic, even incantatory way in which he kills Desdemona – all have seemed to contribute to a racially determined characterization. Thus in a footnote A. C. Bradley nudges the reader of his *Shakespearean Tragedy* towards a recognition of Othello as an excitable African:

> If the reader has ever chanced to see an African violently excited, he may have been startled to observe how completely at a loss he was to interpret those bodily expressions of passion which in a fellow countryman he understands at once, and in a European foreigner with somewhat less certainty. The effect of difference in blood in increasing Othello's bewilderment regarding his wife is not sufficiently realised.[33]

F. R. Leavis suggests that, under Iago's diabolic tutelage, 'Othello's inner timbers begin to part at once, the stuff of which he is made begins at once to deteriorate and show itself unfit'.[34] In his New Cambridge edition of the play, Norman Sanders praises Olivier's definitive rendition of the role: 'this actor produced a virtuoso solo performance that etched a portrait of a primitive man, at odds with the sophisticated society into which he has forced himself, relapsing into barbarism as a result of hideous misjudgement.'[35] Jack D'Amico discusses the play as a tragedy in which

> a man is brought to see himself as he believes others, including his wife, see him. What he sees is 'the Moor', the type set within the social perspectives of Venice. And, tragically, his inability to see himself as anything other than that Moor becomes a kind of proof that the negative image is not a mere illusion, and that what we had taken to be the noble man was, perhaps, something we as spectators imagined, as Desdemona imagined a certain man when she heard him tell his life story.[36]

This account suggests uncomfortably that we have been duped into suspending our knowledge of the operative stereotype: we allowed ourselves to forget the inevitable consequences of Othello's blackness. In all these critical cases some uncontrollable passion constructed as racially and racistly intrinsic recurs when Othello is plunged into jealousy and into an atavistic, uncivilized viciousness. As Michael Neill summarizes, 'if the dominant nineteenth-century tradition sought to domesticate the play by removing the embarrassment of savagery [through cutting], the most common twentieth-century strategy has been to anthropomorphize it as the study of an assimilated savage who relapses into primitivism under stress'.[37]

When Jonathan Miller directed the white actor Anthony Hopkins as Othello for the BBC television series, he maintained that he 'did not see the play as being about colour, but as being about jealousy, which is something we are all vulnerable to'.[38] That race is particular and jealousy universal might itself be seen as a racially inflected observation, and, in any case, Miller's has been a very minority view. That there is some disturbing connection between 'colour' and murderous 'jealousy' is the insidious suggestion the play continues to make, and it is a suggestion that has been elaborated in quite distinct ways. For some critics, Othello's insane jealousy needs to be explained in an essentialist way, as the biological inheritance of a Moor. Leo Africanus's description of the people of Barbary included the comment that 'no nation in the world is so subject unto jealousy; for they will rather lease their lives, than put up any disgrace in the behalf of their women'.[39] This is the racist view that a black man is less in control of his emotions than a white man, and that these cultural aspects of personality are in fact biologically and racially determined. A. W. Schlegel's view of Othello expresses this:

> We recognise in Othello the wild nature of the glowing zone which generates the most ravenous beasts of prey and the most deadly poisons, tamed only in appearance by the desire of fame, by foreign laws of honour, and by nobler and milder manners. His jealousy is not the jealousy of the heart, which is compatible with the tenderest feeling and adoration of the beloved object; it is of that sensual kind which, in burning climes, has given birth to the disgraceful confinement of women and other unnatural usages.[40]

Another way of interpreting the connection between Othello's jealousy and his race is to see it as the contextual property of the outsider. Thus Othello is made jealous by an Iago who preys on his weakness, his feelings of insecurity as a foreigner marked out in a sophisticated and urbane city state such as Venice. Othello's jealousy is thus part of the fact that he is black, but not because this is biologically determined but because it is culturally determined. As Paul Robeson glossed it, 'it is because he is an alien among white people that his mind works as quickly, for he feels dishonour more deeply',[41] giving the play psychological accuracy as the depiction of the life of an outsider.

Related to these different essentialist views of Othello's colour is an interesting and significant shift in the play's stage history. We know that, when Richard Burbage played the leading role in the first years of the seventeenth century, in the absence of any black actor in the King's Men, he probably wore black make-up and a wiry wig. These prosthetics serve immediately to establish race as a matter of theatrical props. As Dympna Callaghan has discussed, this Othello was a white man, his blackness located in cosmetics and thus stressing race as 'representation – that is, as an (anti) aesthetic as opposed to an essence'.[42] The theatrical tradition of white actors blacking up to play Othello continued through the Restoration and beyond. James Quin, performing the role in the eighteenth century, provoked a racial frisson when he peeled off white gloves to reveal the blacked hand beneath.[43] Black actors in the role begin with Ira Aldridge in the nineteenth century, but it is the landmark performance of Paul Robeson in the 1930s that inaugurates a tradition in which blackface Othellos have been largely replaced by black actors. Seeing Robeson as Othello was, for John Dover Wilson, like 'seeing the tragedy for the first time':

> the fact that he was a true Negro seemed to floodlight the whole drama. Everything was slightly different from what I had previously imagined; new points, fresh nuances, were constantly emerging; and all had, I felt, been clearly intended by the author. The performance convinced me in short that a Negro Othello is essential to the full understanding of the play.[44]

Ruth Cowhig has echoed: 'I only want to see black actors in the part.'[45] Black actors including John Kani, Willard White, Laurence Fishburne and Ray Fearon have since played notable Othellos in a theatrical climate that may support 'colour-blind' casting in other roles but has largely decided that Othello should be played only by black actors. The stereotypical and demeaning associations of minstrel-show blacking up have been jettisoned by a liberal theatrical culture inclined to stress the specificity of 'Othello' over the stereotype 'Moor'.

Recently, however, there has been something of a shift. Hugh Quarshie, a black actor with the Royal Shakespeare Company, has written of this new assumption:

I am left with a nagging doubt: if a black actor plays Othello does he not risk making racial stereotypes seem legitimate and even true? When a black actor plays a role written for a white actor in black make-up and for a predominantly white audience, does he not encourage the white way, or rather the wrong way, of looking at black men, namely that black men, or 'Moors', are over-emotional, excitable and unstable, thereby vindicating Iago's statement, 'These Moors are changeable in their wills' (1.3.346). Of all the parts in the canon, perhaps Othello is the one which should most definitely not be played by a black actor.[46]

Quarshie's point is that a black actor gives a credibility, an authenticity, to the role of Othello that serves to corroborate the play's own prejudices. Two notable productions have attempted to play out Quarshie's logic in two different ways, each trying to denaturalize the play's tendency towards essentialism when a black actor plays the central role.

The first is Jude Kelly's so-called 'photo-negative' production in Washington in 1997 with a white Othello, Patrick Stewart, amid a largely black cast. The language remained the same, thus separating racial insults like 'thicklips' from their apparent signifieds to denaturalize bigoted perceptions. Interviewed in the *Washington Post*, Kelly suggested that this casting unsettled racial assumptions for liberal audiences, just as Shakespeare had intended: 'What's fascinating for me is that you have 22 African American actors onstage who know what racism is about, and one white British actor who may know the effects of racism but has never experienced it the way they have. So the images of racial hostility flip back and forth. What it all means, I think, will depend very much on the color of the person who's watching'.[47] The imagery of flipping again recalls the game 'Othello': rather than dismantling the black-white binary of the play, Kelly's production showed how it could be flipped and reversed, severing racist ties with supposed empirical observation and demonstrating the arbitrariness of conventional racial classification. Reviewers were divided about whether the production erased race or foregrounded it, but one critic argues compellingly that it 'asked questions about race in America, and the limits and stereotypes associated with blackness'.[48]

If Kelly's production attempted to challenge a complacently liberal theatre audience through racial cross-casting, a production by the radical German director Peter Zadek tried something rather different. In Hamburg in 1976 he cast a white actor, Ulrich Wildgruber, in obvious and parodic black minstrel make-up. Wildgruber 'deliberately played Othello on the surface, underscoring the cliché and therefore deconstructing it'. Wearing a King Kong costume, Wildgruber repeatedly *performed* stereotypes of blackness rather than attempting to personate them. His black make-up smudged all over Desdemona (Eva Mattes) in the murder scene, 'a parody of a sex crime' and a 'pandemonium of comic terror'. The aim was to shock audiences, and to go 'beyond traditional psychology into the realm of cultural myth and cultural fear'.[49] Zadek's Othello was self-evidently not a black man but a white projection of racist fears and typologies of blackness: Quarshie's unease at a black actor inevitably endorsing and authenticating the portrayal of the Moor is here entirely, albeit uncomfortably, calmed. A blackface Othello must always ironize the racial essentialism of the biblical proverb of impossibility 'to wash the Ethiop white', since it will always be evident that after the final curtain he will indeed wash off his assumed blackness. By returning the role of Othello to a white impersonation, by stressing that it is as much about a historically and culturally specific idea of the 'Moor' as about the tragic individual 'Othello', the play in the theatre can work to unsettle rather than enforce the racial stereotyping with which it has always been consciously and unwittingly associated.

48

3

The Domestic Sphere

The staging of the play's final act represents the culmination of its thematic and visual chiaroscuro, as Othello's black skin and Emilia's racialized outrage at 'the blacker devil' (5.2.140) contrast with the 'monumental alabaster' (5.2.5) of Desdemona among the white sheets of the bed. It is also the place where the private domestic world – the relationship between Othello and Desdemona symbolized by its intimate location – becomes public. There are an increasing number of people crammed into the small space of the bedchamber in Act 5 Scene 2, as Emilia, Iago, Montano, Graziano, Lodovico, Cassio and 'officers' all pile into their debased privacy. Othello's suicide is figured not as an act of private remorse. Nor is he subjected to the local, familial quest for revenge that Desdemona's relatives enact in Cinthio's *Hecatommithi*. Cinthio's story culminates with the brutal murder of Disdemona by the Moor and the Ensign armed with 'a stocking filled with sand'. According to their plan, the Ensign is hidden 'in a closet which opened off the bedchamber'. While husband and wife are in bed together he contrives to make a noise, and, when Disdemona is sent by the Moor to investigate, she is repeatedly and fatally bludgeoned by his accomplice. When she is dead, they pull the ceiling of the bedchamber onto her body to disguise her murder: 'when she is dead,' advises the Ensign, 'we shall make part of the ceiling fall; and we'll break the Lady's head, making it seem that a rafter has injured it in falling, and killed her. In this way, everyone will think she died accidentally.'[1] For Cinthio's story, the destruction of the bedchamber is thus first a practical, if ineffectual, gesture of concealment; but the image also functions metaphorically to indicate the destruction of the home, the domestic and sexual sphere of the married couple. The taint of jealousy has destroyed the physical fabric of domestic life, bringing down the rafters of their broken relationship onto the defiled bed. The image of domestic rubble symbolizes a crushed marriage, but it may also nod towards the structure of tragic narrative itself. Philip Sidney, writing in his *Defence of Poesie* in the 1580s, describes the didactic effects of tragedy in terms derived from the 'pity and fear' of Aristotle's *Poetics*, but with a particular architectural twist: tragedy, by 'stirring the affects of admiration and commiseration, teacheth the uncertainty of this world, and upon how weak foundations gilden roofs are builded'.[2]

It is immediately evident that Shakespeare has made a number of important changes to this section of his source. In *Othello*, Iago's absence from the scene of Desdemona's murder is a significant indication of just how far he has led Othello 'by th' nose/ As asses are' (1.3.393–4); rather than being the agent of her death, he has prompted Othello to kill her himself: 'strangle her in her bed, even the bed she hath contaminated' (4.1.202–3). In common with its repeated pattern of conjugal interruption in which the couple are disturbed from their bed, the play diverges from the source in having Desdemona alone in her wedding sheets when Othello comes to dispatch her. Othello's actions seem to refigure the killing as a ritual sacrifice: he chooses to smother or strangle his wife rather than beat her, despite numerous earlier suggestions that she will be stabbed ('Thy bed, lust-stained, shall with lust's blood be spotted' (5.1.37)). Nor is there any real attempt to conceal her body or the events of the murder, other than the curtaining of the bed. In literal terms the chamber is still intact at the end of the play. In metaphorical terms, however, Shakespeare thoroughly integrates into his play Cinthio's image of the tumbling ceiling and the destruction of the domestic space. Derogated images of 'home', 'house' and 'lodging', and a systematic disparaging of the domestic world, combine to establish its loss as one of the causes and casualties of the tragedy. But, whereas domestic destruction is the endpoint of Cinthio's narrative, in Shakespeare it is the starting point. Rather than leading up to an image of domestic loss, Shakespeare shows us that, from its opening scene, this play was always and already post-domestic.

Othello has often been identified with the subgenre of late Elizabethan and early Jacobean plays known as 'domestic tragedy'. These plays, grouped around the turn of the century, usually concern protagonists of middle, non-noble rank set in recognizably domestic, often small-town provincial settings – the bourgeois house in Faversham in *Arden of Faversham* (*c.*1591), the gentry household in Heywood's *A Woman Killed with Kindness* (1603) – and preoccupied with the minutiae of daily living. Stage directions in Heywood's play establish the domestic setting with detailed props: '*Enter 3 or 4 Servingmen, one with a voider and a wooden knife to take away all; another the salt and bread; another the tablecloth and napkins; another the carpet.*' Arden is murdered during a game of backgammon by assassins who hide in his counting-house to await their opportunity.[3] Domestic tragedies usually dramatize female transgression that splits apart the household: both *Arden of Faversham* and *A Warning for Fair Women* (*c.*1590) dramatize a young wife and her lover murdering her husband, and *A Woman Killed with Kindness* tells of Anne Frankford's adultery. Recent work on these plays has identified in their particular household settings significant interrogations of late Tudor domestic ideology, as they dramatize 'ways in which the patriarchal center did not always hold'.[4] As women took control of the household as part of the new Protestant ideologies of gendered roles within a companionate marriage, the idea of the home as man's dominion, securely within the compass of patriarchal power, was under increasing threat. Many critics have read domestic tragedies alongside the conduct books and household management books that were widely printed and reprinted in the Elizabethan and Jacobean periods, as parallel documents attesting to the complex and shifting roles of men and women in the household, and the ongoing analogical attempt to conceive of household order as a microcosm of state government. According to this model of correspondences, as Katherine puts it at the end of *The Taming of the Shrew*, 'such duty as the subject owes the prince/ Even as such a woman oweth to her husband' (5.2.160–1).

Like other plays identified with the genre, *Othello* can be seen as essentially 'domestic' in tone and scope. It deals not with kings and princes but with the daughter of a Venetian citizen and the former-slave turned general. Bradley argues it is 'less unlike a story of private life than any other of the great tragedies', and A. D. Nuttall identifies it as an example of 'the tragedy of private, household events' as opposed to the 'tragedy of courts'.[5] As Thomas Rymer noted with considerable scorn in the seventeenth century, its plot turns on that most mundane and trivial of domestic props, the handkerchief, and he derives a series of bathetic morals from the story to emphasize his disparagement of its inappropriately sub-tragic scope:

> First, This may be a caution to all Maidens of Quality how, without their Parents consent, they run away with *Blackamoors*. ...
> Secondly, This may be a warning to all good Wives that they look well to their Linnen.
> Thirdly, This may be a lesson to Husbands, that before their Jealousie be Tragical the proofs may be Mathematical.[6]

Dympna Callaghan echoes Rymer's perception of this 'Tragedy of [a] *Trifle*' when she calls the play 'embarrassingly domestic'; George Bernard Shaw concurs, describing the play as a 'splendid melodrama' with 'its police-court morality and commonplace thought'.[7]

As in the examples of domestic tragedy discussed above, *Othello* can be situated amid material domestic props: Stanley Wells describes the 'wealth of social detail' in Trevor Nunn's 1989 production at Stratford (much of the stage business is preserved in the filmed version of this production adapted for television by David Myerscough-Jones in 1990). 'A fully written account of this production would read like a Victorian novel,' writes Wells, as he picks out campbeds, a telescope on the Cyprus quayside, and Iago pocketing a cigar left on the council table as examples.[8] Virginia Vaughan quotes from Edmund Kean's props list for his early nineteenth-century production: 'Couch, or sofa R[ight]. Scrolls for Othello. Table & Chair L[eft]. Footstool in front. Book on Table. Strawberry spotted H Kerchief for Desdemona.' A spectator described Act 5 of the production with 'everything in the proper order: she wears a nightcap and lies covered with a quilt. There is a curtain over the bed and beside it a little stool, a night table; they even said that a chamber pot could be seen under the bed.'[9] Jonathan Miller's television production for the BBC (1981) uses no exterior shots, showing us only a glimpse of the sea through a window in the storm scene: much of the action is set amid 'a maze of rooms and hallways within the fortress'[10] with a concentration on carefully lit domestic interiors that reminded some critics of Dutch artists such as Vermeer.

In addition, unlike most of Shakespeare's tragedies that move to suggest that the downfall of the central protagonist has a wider moral, political or epistemological significance, here in *Othello* there is relatively little suggestion of a wider metaphysical correspondence for the play's events. There is no Prologue telling us of 'star-crossed lovers' (*Romeo and Juliet*); no cosmic juxtaposition of man and nature as in Lear's rantings on the stormy heath; no cannibalistic horses or overturned natural hierarchies as after the murder of Duncan in *Macbeth*; no lions whelp in the streets to presage the death of Desdemona as they do in *Julius Caesar*. Indeed, Othello draws attention to the bathos of such absence:

> O heavy hour!
> Methinks it should be now a huge eclipse
> Of sun and moon, and that th'affrighted globe
> Should yawn at alteration.

(5.2.107–10)

The agony of the end of the play is accompanied not by cosmic pathetic fallacy but by the mundane interruptions of bewildered bystanders. Jan Kott suggests that these lines reveal *Othello* as 'the tragedy of a man under an empty heaven'.[11] The scale of this play about the catastrophic breakdown of trust is human rather than divine, private rather than public, domestic rather than cosmic.

But *Othello*'s structure diverges significantly from the trajectory of domestic tragedy in its depiction of the domestic sphere. Here the household functions not as the locus of social and sexual transgression: rather it is the loss of the domestic setting, and the ongoing ambivalence to this form of familial containment, which sets in motion the tragedy.

Nuttall describes the genre of *Othello* as 'strangely – and formally – introverted: it consists in the fact that [Othello] left the arena proper to tragedy, the battlefield, and entered a subtragic world for which he was not fitted. *Othello* is the story of a hero who went into a house.'[12] Nuttall's juxtaposition of house and battlefield is a suggestive one for the themes and structure of *Othello*, and one with which the warrior Othello

53

himself, who maintains that 'little of this great world can I speak/ More than pertains to feats of broil and battle' (1.3.86–7), might agree. However, he overstates the case. To be sure, Othello does leave the battlefield, but he never fully does go into a house, never conforms himself to that domestic space. In fact it is the absence of the domestic, rather than the domestic space itself, that is tragic in *Othello*. This is a 'domestic tragedy' that has, from the outset, slipped its domestic moorings, and that lodges uncertainly in the non-domestic, the post-domestic, the 'unhoused', and in what Freud calls the uncanny or *unheimlich* (literally 'unhomely'). From the very start, domestic containment is hollowed out into disconcertingly 'wheeling' (1.1.138) social and personal instability.

This theme is established in the opening moments of the play. *Othello* begins with a commotion in the street outside Brabanzio's house. Iago tells Roderigo to 'Call up her father,/ Rouse him, make after him, poison his delight,/ Proclaim him in the streets; incense her kinsmen' (1.1.67–9). Iago rouses Brabanzio with a warning designed to appeal to the Venetian householder: 'thieves, thieves!/ Look to your house, your daughter, and your bags' (1.1.79–80). The stage direction has Brabanzio appear 'at a window above', probably the balcony on the tiring house wall that formed the back of the Globe stage. Roderigo asks him 'is all your family within?'(1.1.84), and Iago, 'Are your doors locked?' (1.1.85). Roderigo explains to the man who has charged him 'not to haunt about my doors' (1.1.97) that another, unseen and unhindered, has stolen away his daughter. Brabanzio feels that his house, 'not a grange' (1.1.108) or isolated homestead but a city dwelling, is safe. Desdemona, however, has 'made a gross revolt' (1.1.136) in eloping by public transport to her lover. 'How got she out?' (1.1.171) asks her enraged and bewildered father. The theft of his daughter is a theft of property: the word 'jewel' is used ironically by Brabanzio in 1.3.194 to address his escaped and deflowered daughter. As the play begins, therefore, the sleeping house has been broached, penetrated: the integrity of the household broken apart.

In an influential essay 'Patriarchal Territories', Peter Stallybrass discusses the Renaissance topos of *hortus conclusus*. This imagery of closed, sealed spaces conceptualizes women as 'the enclosed body, the closed mouth, the locked house', and allows us to make the connection between the enclosed but vulnerable household and the enclosed and vulnerable woman. Stallybrass suggests that patriarchal 'surveillance of women concentrated upon three specific areas: the mouth, chastity, the threshold of the house',[13] homologous sites that frequently collapsed into each other. The analogy suggests that Brabanzio's breached house is a figure for the lost intactness of Desdemona herself, 'making the beast with two backs' (1.1.118–19) in some unknown and undomestic location with her lover. As Stallybrass explores, the topos of closedness is mirrored with the ever-present threat of its breach: the woman is 'that treasure which, however locked up, always escapes'. Brabanzio's ransacked house thus figures metaphorically as that which cannot be literally depicted: the occluded sexual act with which the play is so insistently concerned, and to which it returns, again in metaphor, in the play's parallel concluding scene when another bedchamber is disturbed by a commotion outside. This time, however, we are disconcertingly within the chamber, not without.

The metaphor of the house for female virginity echoes the depiction of another elopement in another Venetian play much concerned with fathers, daughters and miscegenation, *The Merchant of Venice*. Here the Jewish Shylock returns home to find that Jessica, the daughter to whom he has given his keys and instructed 'Look to my house' (2.5.16), has run off with her Christian lover Lorenzo. In *The Merchant of Venice*, as in *Othello*, the view of the patriarch that the house is a place of security under masculine control has been shattered, revealed as a hollow complacency. The house is already empty before the play begins, and the irrevocable separation of the female from the domestic is the starting point for the tragedy. Oliver Parker's film begins with shadowy figures in silent gondolas on the canal, and then shows us Desdemona, veiled, disembarking from a gondola and rushing through the night streets still scattered with the refuse from the food market, thus displacing the sense of her escape and, perhaps, more obliquely, a hint at her sexual pollution into the exterior landscape of the night streets.

That women were normatively associated with household duties and the domestic sphere in conduct literature of the period is a commonplace. In Richard Dod and John Cleaver's

1598 conduct book *A Godly form of household Government*, the authors observe that 'a modest and chaste woman that loveth her husband must also love her house, as remembering that the husband that loveth his wife, cannot so well like the sight of any tapestry as to see his wife in his house'. Henry Smith's sermon on marriage published in 1591 argued that 'we call the wife *housewife* ... to show that a good wife keeps her house ... it becometh her to keep home'. In his didactic poem of 1617, Samuel Rowland enumerates the duties of the bride:

> The first is that she have domestic cares
> Of private business for the house within,
> Leaving her husband unto his affairs,
> Of things abroad that out of doors have been
> By him performed, as his charge to do,
> Not busy-body like inclined thereto.[14]

These repeated iterations attempt to establish marital containment within the domestic sphere as the sign and corollary of obedient and chaste femininity.

Othello's autobiography of his courtship of Desdemona in her father's house makes clear that, from the start, their relationship was always in tension with her duties in the home. While he was invited into the domestic space by Brabanzio – 'her father loved me, oft invited me' (1.3.127) – the effect of his presence has been to destroy that domesticity from within. Desdemona hurried through the unwelcome 'house affairs' (1.3.146), the domestic duties that kept her from Othello's company, in order to return to his stories of the wild landscape: 'antres vast and deserts idle,/ Rough quarries, rocks, and hills whose heads touch heaven' (1.3.139-40). Desdemona was wooed from her father's home through words rather than Othello's looks. Eager for more of these glamorous stories, she would 'with a greedy ear/ Devour up my discourse' (1.3.148–9). Images of appetite cast this dereliction of the normative domestic female role as a physical response; the open ear, imagined as a devouring mouth, functions as a synecdoche for her responsive body, seduced by exotic (literally 'outside') stories – and introduce the theme of food and appetite, which is discussed below as an index of domestic debasement during the play.

In preference to her own home and her domestic obligations to her presumably widowed father, Desdemona has allied herself with a man repeatedly identified as rootless or displaced. All Renaissance marriages – a feature retained today by the traditional Christian marriage ceremony, where the bride is given away by her father or other male relative – entailed the transmission of the daughter from her father's household to that of her husband: indeed, Desdemona uses this precedent to persuade her reluctant father that his opposition to their marriage is unreasonable, drawing on the example of her absent mother who 'preferr[ed] you before her father' (1.3.186). But, strikingly, the couple do not spend their wedding night under Othello's roof, where the Duke's messengers seek him, but instead at the Sagittary, apparently an inn or lodging house. Desdemona's passage is not from her father's to her husband's, but out of the fixed and enclosed Venetian domestic sphere into a world that is literally unhoused. When he is dispatched by the Duke and Council to Cyprus, Othello's first thought is for 'such accommodation and besort/As levels with her breeding' (1.3.237–8) for Desdemona in his absence: as soldier-husband, he has no permanent household of his own in which to install her. The Duke's suggestion that she return to her father's is not a possibility for either Brabanzio or Othello, both of whom reject it out of hand. The domestic is thus lost forever to Desdemona, as she has chosen to leave her father's protection. To emphasize the irreversibility of the step, at the end of the play Graziano tells of Brabanzio's death: 'Thy match was mortal to him, and pure grief/ Shore his old thread in twain' (5.2.212–13). Perhaps this unexpected elegy is designed to elevate Brabanzio's opposition to the match from bigotry into paternal heartbreak, and to emphasize, as the play reaches its closing moments, the destructive power of this unorthodox marriage.

Thus, while Desdemona 'did love the Moor to live with him'(1.3.248), where that new abode will be is by no means clear. The failure to establish a household for his marriage is not merely a bachelor oversight by Othello. Rather, it is crucial to his characterization. As we have already seen, 'the Moor of Venice', as insisted on by the play's subtitle and the running title on early printed texts, is already paradoxical, defined by geographical displacement and non-belonging. This may be a quality the play connects to his racial identity: Leo Africanus describes Africans as 'being most ignorant of natural, domestical, and commonwealth-manners', adding that they 'observe no certain order of living nor of laws'.[15] Roderigo calls Othello 'extravagant', which, with its etymological links to vagrancy, denotes roaming and unfixedness, and 'wheeling' (1.1.138) also suggestive of giddiness and perpetual motion. Iago's description of Othello as 'erring barbarian' (1.3.354) also activates the meanings of 'erring' as 'wandering, straying' as well as 'mistaken' or 'wrong'. The contrast between these epithets and the image of the outraged householder Brabanzio woken from his bourgeois bed and emerging, as the quarto text stage direction states, in his 'nightgown', is pointed.

For Roderigo and Iago these insinuations of the nomadic are intended as derogatory, but Othello claims for himself a similar itinerant status:

> But that I love the gentle Desdemona
> I would not my unhousèd free condition
> Put into circumscription and confine
> For the seas' worth.
>
> (1.2.25–8)

Othello imagines marriage as constriction, as fixity, as a kind of diminution – and his ambivalence towards this new constraint is crucial to the play. 'Unhoused' here is Shakespeare's first usage of this negative (the only other is in *Timon of Athens*) – and it represents that absolute confounding of ideas of the domestic that is begun in the play's opening scene and that continues throughout. Othello describes his own adventures in the 'tented field' (1.3.85); the temporary military encampments are implicitly contrasted with the stones and mortar of the Venetian war council. Like Antony in *Antony and Cleopatra*, this soldier disdains the comforts of home: he is used to making 'the flinty and steel couch of war/ My thrice-driven bed of down' (1.3.229–30).

Even the 'couch of war' is not to be found in this play of thwarted militarism. Rather, Desdemona's flight from her father's home initiates a focus on temporary dwelling places. 'Home' is an absence, underlined by its ironic use when Iago instructs Roderigo about the attack on Cassio: 'Wear thy good rapier bare, and put it home' (5.1.2). The word 'home' really only resurfaces at the end of the play, when it refers to the lost Venice to which the characters will never return, as when

Othello reads the commission from the senate: 'I am commanded home' (4.1.260). In place of this lost home, we have a succession of debased substitutes: the Sagittary, military lodgings, 'where thou art billeted' (2.3.370), and the citadel. Iago has his own 'lodging' (1.3.372) in Venice and presumably some shared accommodation with Emilia in Cyprus – the 'home' he threatens her with in the final act – and yet his claim that 'I lay with Cassio lately' (3.3.418) is at least plausible to Othello. Cassio found the handkerchief in his 'chamber' (3.4.185), but many productions have envisaged a barrack-room camaraderie between the soldiery that supports the male bonding crucial to the play's emotional dynamic. In the filmed version of Trevor Nunn's production, for example, Iago busies himself with folding the blankets on the campbeds and improvising a punchbowl for the drinking scene from a tin ewer.

The connotations of temporariness that attach themselves to the word 'lodging' – used in connection with Othello, Iago and Cassio – are in implicit contradistinction to the word 'house' associated with Brabanzio, and, in her transgression, with Desdemona. 'Lodging' has a number of suggestive connotations. The *Oxford English Dictionary* gives a range of early modern meanings including 'hired rooms' and, more specifically, 'bedroom' (*OED* 4.a), 'portion of space assigned to one man in a [military] camp' (*OED* 4.b), and, nicely for our gaming metaphor, 'a square on a chess-board' (*OED* 4.d). When Desdemona talks with the Clown about where Cassio may be found (3.4), the repeated punning on 'lies' and 'lodges' further associates the term with deceit, uncertainty, shiftiness and, tacitly, sexuality and penetration. By the time the plot has moved to Cyprus, the idea of 'house' has been denigrated: in common with *Measure for Measure*, written contemporaneously, 'house' here may suggest the commodification of female sexuality in Bianca's 'house' (3.4.168, 5.1.121); alternatively it may establish Bianca as the only woman allied within a domestic, albeit unhusbanded, sphere. For Othello, 'house' entraps infection rather than protecting from it:

> it comes o'er my memory
> As doth the raven o'er the infectious house,
> Boding to all!

> (4.1.20–2)

59

The extent to which this domestic tragedy has become undomesticated has its psychic parallel in Freud's essay on the quality he called 'The Uncanny', or, in German, 'Das Unheimliche' (the unhomely). The uncanny is characterized as 'related to what is frightening – to what arouses dread and horror', terms that are particularly relevant to a tragedy that prompts 'mingled emotions of consternation, disgust and grief. You feel as if you had seen a murder or attended an execution.'[16] Freud argues that the connotations of *heimlich*, or 'homely', threaten to spill into its apparent opposite, *unheimlich*, or uncanny: 'the uncanny is that class of the frightening which leads back to what is known of old and long familiar',[17] just as it is the closed door of the bedroom behind which Othello imagines the most monstrous of events. Freud's characterization of the uncanny has a number of other suggestive resonances for *Othello*. Aspects of the uncanny also include doubts about whether an apparently animate being is really alive, the uncanny aspect of epileptic fits, which offers a way of integrating an aspect of Othello's characterization that is not found in Cinthio and that directors and actors have long found problematic in its melodrama.[18] Often the uncanny is connected to a lack of agency. Freud quotes an earlier essay by Ernst Jentsch: 'in telling a story, one of the most successful devices for creating uncanny effects is to leave the reader in uncertainty whether a particular figure in the story is a human being or an automaton'[19] – this is a feature of the deterministic logic of the tragic outcome discussed in the next chapter on genre. Finally, Freud discusses how 'an uncanny effect is often and easily produced when the distinction between imagination and reality is effaced, as when ... a symbol takes over the full functions of the thing it symbolizes'.[20] It is hard to think of a clearer example than that of the handkerchief in Othello's poisoned mind, which becomes the 'lust-spotted sheets' seemingly corroborated by its apparent transmission to Cassio.

The play's suspicion of interior spaces as places of hidden deceit grows: after talking about catching the pair *in flagrante*, Iago pushes Othello's mind towards the door of their adulterous chamber:

> If imputation, and strong circumstances
> Which lead directly to the door of truth,

Will give you satisfaction, you might ha't.

(3.3.411–13)

This 'door' resurfaces in Othello's mind as he accuses Emilia of bawding: 'Leave procreants alone and shut the door' (4.2.30) and describes her as 'a subtle whore,/ A closet lock and key of villainous secrets' (4.2.22–3); Iago encourages Othello to torture himself with images of a 'kiss in private':

> There's millions now alive
> That nightly lie in those unproper beds
> Which they dare swear peculiar.
>
> .   .   .   .   .
>
> To lip a wanton in a secure couch
> And to suppose her chaste!

(4.1.66–71)

Illicit sex is associated with a terrible fertility as Othello imagines these adulterous 'procreants' behind closed doors. Whereas prominent in the last act of *Titus Andronicus* is a mixed-race baby born of the liaison between Aaron the Moor and his Goth lover Tamora, in *Othello* the impossibility of Desdemona and Othello's marriage means that pregnancy, too, is impossible. Iago plays on Brabanzio's fear that 'the devil will make a grandsire of you' (1.1.91), but these fears are tragically subverted. This is a liaison that results in unparenting, in the denial of fatherly affection to his child: 'I had rather to adopt a child than get it' (1.3.196) – and one that will end in death, including Brabanzio's own, rather than in new life. There are other indications of sterility, too. In Cinthio's source story, the Ensign has a 'little girl of three years old'[21] who provides the diversion necessary for him to steal Disdemona's handkerchief: Iago has no children, and, instead, images of conception and gestation are wrested from physical reproduction into the grotesque fecundity of his plotting: 'I ha't. It is ingendered. Hell and night/ Must bring this monstrous birth to the world's light' (1.3.395–6). Often the relationship between stage Emilias and Iagos has been suggestive of sexual frustration: Kenneth Tynan wrote of Frank Finlay, Iago to Olivier's Othello, that 'he has been impotent for years – hence his loathing of Othello's sexuality and his alienation from Emilia'.[22] That this denial of marital affection may indicate repressed homosexual feelings, and that these may form part of Iago's

61

opaque motivations, has often been suggested. For example, Finlay as Iago straddled Othello as he lay on the ground in his trance in Act 4, Scene 1, thrusting the handle of his dagger into his victim's mouth; and the scene in Parker's film in which Iago and Roderigo discuss their plots lying under a cart on which a couple are energetically copulating is cited by Richard Burt in support of his interpretation that Branagh plays Iago as 'a gay man who loves Othello but cannot admit it, and so destroys him and his wife'.[23]

The edgy, wry exchanges between Desdemona and Iago in Cyprus as they wait for news of Othello's safe passage through the storm often turn on their joint derogation of the domestic sphere. Iago derides women in specifically domestic terms:

> You are pictures out of door,
> Bells in your parlours; wildcats in your kitchens,
> Saints in your injuries; devils being offended,
> Players in your housewifery, and housewives in your beds
>
> (2.1.112–15)

associating housewifery with pretence and with sexual, rather than household, labours. (This quotation follows the Folio reading: the Oxford edition's emendation of 'housewives' to 'hussies' privileges the sexual aspect of the pun over the domestic.) Elsewhere the title 'housewife' is a term of abuse. When Desdemona requests permission to accompany her husband to war, Othello fears marriage as effeminization, or rather fears that others will view this as effeminization: if 'my disports corrupt and taint my business,/ Let housewives make a skillet of my helm' (1.3.271–2). In the image of the warrior's helmet redeployed as a small cooking pot, the domestic, here associated with the sexual 'disports', threatens to diminish the masculine ego: Othello's mistrust of domesticity is revealed. Later he speaks contemptuously of 'chamberers' – Shakespeare's only use of the word, meaning gallant or 'one who frequents ladies' chambers' (*OED* 4) – having 'soft parts of conversation' (3.3.268): men accommodated within the household sphere are treated with derision. When Iago calls Bianca 'A housewife that by selling her desires/ Buys herself bread and cloth' (4.1.93–4), fear of women and the utter semantic denigration of 'housewife' is complete. (The Oxford edition's emendation to 'hussy' makes the point clear.) Even his mock-eulogy of the female sex at Desdemona's request ends with Iago's bathetic identification of women with trivial household economy. Iago's ironic female paragon is ultimately fit to 'suckle fools, and chronicle small beer' (2.1.163) – fit for the conventional roles of mother and domestic manager. Desdemona herself has inter-nalized this negative view of the female domestic role, promising to act the shrew in prosecuting Cassio's cause with her husband: 'I'll watch him tame, and talk him out of patience,/ His bed shall seem a school, his board a shrift' (3.3.23–4). She does not seem to realize that this image of domestic imprisonment, marriage as educational and religious restriction, is part of what Othello most fears from his new status.

Images of food and appetite, literal and symbolic, mark the breakdown of Othello and Desdemona's marriage. From the exotic menu of the 'cannibals that each other eat' (1.3.142), part of the repertoire of winning stories from their courtship, to Iago's insistence on sexual love as mere appetite – 'Her eye must be fed' (2.1.226) – food, its rituals and its consumption offer an index to the health of their domestic relationship. Images of shared meals and the activity of eating are part of their routine. 'Full liberty of feasting' (2.2.9) is pronounced as the island's joint celebration of their deliverance from the Turks and the marriage of their general. As in many other domestic tragedies, shared food acts as an image for conjugal living. When Othello tries to defend himself against Iago's insinuations, he inserts the verb 'feeds' into what could otherwise be a conventional catalogue of female attributes: ' 'Tis not to make me jealous/ To say my wife is fair, feeds well, loves company,/ Is free of speech, sings, plays, and dances well' (3.3.187–9), and he echoes this image in his own pre-jealous oblivion: 'I saw't not, thought it not; it harmed not me./ I slept the night well, fed well, was free and merry' (3.3.344–5).

Desdemona tries to use their shared board as a forum to reinstate Cassio in her husband's favour. Othello's refusal – 'I shall not dine at home./ I meet the captains at the citadel' (3.3.59–60) – brings her ingenuous response: 'Why then, tomorrow night, or Tuesday morn,/ On Tuesday noon, or night, on Wednesday morn' (3.3.61–2). Her attempts to persuade him are couched in the language of loving domesticity: ''Tis as I should entreat you wear your gloves,/ Or feed on nourishing dishes' (3.3.78–9). Desdemona interrupts the long scene of Iago's manipulation, Act 3 Scene 3, with the mundane call to dinner. Othello remembers himself amid a confused sequence of emotions to call Lodovico and the Venetian emissaries to 'sup together' (4.1.264), and the summons 'to supper' interrupts Iago's feigned comforting of Desdemona (4.2.174).

Increasingly, however, references to feeding are cut loose from the literal, as the play moves inexorably towards Iago's contemptuous view of human motivations as animalistic appetite: 'the food that to him now is as luscious as locusts shall be to him shortly as bitter as coloquintida' (1.3.347–9. Perhaps it is not entirely casual that Iago attributes his attentiveness to Cassio's sleeptalking to a 'raging tooth' (3.3.419). Othello curses marriage 'that we can call these delicate creatures ours/ And not their appetites' (3.3.273–4), and imagines the 'general camp ... had tasted her sweet body' (3.3.350–1): Desdemona has shifted from one who 'feeds well' to one who is consumed, sexually and serially, by others. This sense of consumption is echoed in Othello's dreadful and debased threat 'I will chop her into messes' (4.1.195): the word 'messes' suggests servings of meat, and is connected to his description of her as honest 'as summer flies are in the shambles [slaughter-house],/ That quicken even with blowing' (4.2.68–9). There may be a submerged connection to the cannibalism that featured in his early wooing stories. Abraham Hartwell's *A Report of the Kingdom of Congo*, published in 1597, states that the Congolese 'deliver [their enemies] to the butchers to be cut in pieces, and so sold to be roasted or boiled'.[24] The degraded imagery of food and eating is used extensively by Emilia in her cynical assessment of sexual relationships: 'They are all but stomachs, and we all but food./ They eat us hungrily, and when they are full,/ They belch us' (3.4.102–4), and she echoes this when she claims equality of appetite for women, who 'have their palates both for sweet and sour,/ As husbands have' (4.3.94–5). Peter Hall's 1980 production in London anticipated this connection: in Act 2, Scene 1, as the Venetians came ashore in Cyprus, hot soup was offered to the storm-tossed travellers; Desdemona's refusal of food contrasted sharply with Emilia's greedy display of appetite.[25] In the final scene Othello has 'stomach' for revenge (5.2.82). The ultimate image for this perversion of sustenance is the self-devouring personification of jealousy: 'the green-eyed monster which doth mock/ The meat it feeds on' (3.3.170–1). The figure of the monster has shifted from those exotic and externalized 'cannibals', 'anthropophagi, and men whose heads/ Do grow beneath their shoulders' (1.3.142–4), and has become instead the terrifying, devouring monster within.

The domestic sphere, appetite and sexuality are all seen to be closely connected in a network of allusions to literal and metaphorical eating. Antipathy to the domestic in *Othello* is part of the play's ambivalence towards women and their control over men. An unexplained and problematic part – since Cassio is evidently not married – of Iago's early denigration of the lieutenant describes him as 'almost damned in a fair wife' (1.1.20), which many commentators have attempted to gloss as 'ladies' man' or as 'man almost degraded into a woman',[26] but which also serves prophetically to characterize Othello himself. When one of the gentlemen asks Cassio in Act 2 'is your general wived?' (2.1.61), the form of words seems to suggest not simply that he has taken a wife but that something has been done to him. To be wived is, perhaps, to have the helm taken for a skillet. The counterpart to this is Cassio's statement to Bianca that he does not wish to have Othello 'see me womaned' (3.4.192): the sense that 'womaned' means both 'accompanied by a woman' and 'to become woman-like' may be a direct parallel to the semantic ambiguities of 'wived'. The idea that a married man is in thrall to his wife is repeated. Cassio calls Desdemona 'our great captain's captain' (2.1.75); Iago echoes 'Our general's wife is now the general' (2.3.307–8). As Othello watches, in a kind of ocular equivalent of the bedtrick as presented in contemporaneous plays including *Measure for Measure*, Cassio's disparagement of Bianca serves to vent a more general contempt for women: indeed, it is crucial to the scene that his references to this 'monkey' who 'so hangs and lolls and weeps upon me, so shakes and pulls me – ha, ha, ha!' (4.1.136–7) are interpreted as a reference to Desdemona rather than Bianca. The reception of the play and critics' unthinking acceptance of Iago's depiction of Bianca as a whore provide a counterpart to Othello's quick conviction of Desdemona's adultery. Bianca's own 'I am no strumpet, but of life as honest/ As you that thus abuse me' (5.1.124–5) is parallel to Desdemona's own reply to Othello's

65

'Are not you a strumpet?': 'No, as I am a Christian' (4.2.84–5). Edward Pechter's careful account of the decidedly shaky textual evidence for the Folio text character list's description of Bianca as 'Curtezan' argues that the ease with which this label has stuck on her demonstrates that 'we are still being abused; Iago's poison is still working'.[27] Desdemona, Bianca and Emilia are all called whores during the course of the play: it is a tag that tells us more about the garrison misogyny of the men than about the moral or economic status of the women. Iago plays on Othello's willingness to denigrate all women, as the obverse of his earlier idealization, telling him of Venetian women's sexual 'pranks', and even Emilia seems to confirm this misogynistic idea of voracious female sexual appetite as she dismisses Desdemona's disingenuous surprise at women's unfaithfulness with practised cynicism: 'Marry, I would not do such a thing for a jointring, nor for measures of lawn, nor for gowns, petticoats, nor caps, nor any petty exhibition; but for the whole world?' (4.3.71–4).

Emilia's contrast between small-scale household or domestic props – clothing and jewellery – and the 'whole world' echoes Othello's own abiding sense of the contrast between small and large. In parallel with his literal unhousedness, Othello's language is always striving for liberty and scope. Iago's description of his 'free and open nature' (1.3.391) associates the general with spatial independence, and it is to this fantasy of escape that Othello's language turns at Iago's insidious prompting. When Othello likens his 'bloody thoughts' to

> the Pontic Sea,
> Whose icy current and compulsive course
> Ne'er knows retiring ebb, but keeps due on
> To the Propontic and the Hellespont,

> (3.3.456–9)

he implicitly contrasts marital confinement with the vastness of the ocean. Iago's insinuations about Desdemona's faithfulness bring Othello to a great cry of loss and bereavement, but strikingly it is his soldier's life that is imagined as the casualty of his collapsing marriage:

> I had been happy if the general camp,
> Pioneers and all, had tasted her sweet body,
> So I had nothing known. O, now for ever

> Farewell the tranquil mind, farewell content,
> Farewell the plumèd troops and the big wars
> That makes ambition virtue! O, farewell,
> Farewell the neighing steed and the shrill trump,
> The spirit-stirring drum, th'ear-piercing fife,
> The royal banner, and all quality,
> Pride, pomp, and circumstance of glorious war!
>
> (3.3.350–9)

The speech ends with the heavy finality of 'Farewell! Othello's occupation's gone' (3.3.362) where the word 'occupation' ravels up a connection of passive and active associations. 'Occupation' signals both the act of occupying and the state of being occupied; it has the sense of professional vocation alongside military connotations of invasion and possession, which are also sexualized.[28] It is an image of control and place lost.

Othello's elegy displaces the marital with the martial, and, as Nuttall points out, it is the word 'big' that echoes most: war offers a scope appropriate to Othello's nature, unlike the handkerchief that is 'too little' to bind his headache (3.3.291). As the play proceeds, there is a repeated sense of diminuendo, of a narrowing of Othello's world. The tainted marriage is a prison shared with a rival:

> I had rather be a toad
> And live upon the vapour of a dungeon
> Than keep a corner in the thing I love
> For others' uses.
>
> (3.3.274–7)

Othello recognizes that he has 'garnered up my heart' (4.2.59) – the word 'garnered' comes from 'garner', or grain store and thus is indicative of the emotional and physical constraint of marriage. Othello now finds the space of his relationship a confinement: 'a cistern for foul toads/ To knot and gender in' (4.2.63–4). Jonathan Miller's BBC film anticipated this metaphor with a prominent cistern in Act 1, Scene 1, in which Iago splashes his hands: 'the source whose poisoning of Brabanzio's and later Othello's delight is visually suggested to us as the poisoning of the city's life fountain' – interestingly, an act of social as well as private destruction.[29] Iago promises that he will 'out of [Desdemona's] own goodness make the net/ That shall enmesh them all' (2.3.352–3); 'as little a web as this will ensnare as great a fly as Cassio' (2.1.171–2). Images of imprisonment predominate, from the 'jesses' of the tamed falcon (3.3.265) to the 'yoked' beasts that are married men (4.1.65). Orson Welles's film turns this verbal element into visual poetry. Welles begins his film by intercutting two images of terminal incarceration: the funeral biers of Desdemona and Othello, and the suspended latticework cage in which Iago has been imprisoned. He continues to render pictorially the text's interplay between images of liberty and constraint, between emotional and physical space and crampedness. Scenes cross-hatched with shadow, floors tessellated with tiles, views through the fretwork of barred windows and grills, the mesh of Desdemona's hair snood, images culminating in the crisscross of the open-weave cloth placed over Desdemona's face to smother her – these all serve to translate the verbal into the visual. As Othello looks on at the scene in which Cassio denigrates Bianca, his face is pictured boxed in a tiny aperture in the city walls: Iago's psychological entrapment and his unusual injunction 'encave' (4.1.80) has its physical counterpart. It may be that readers of the play share with its central protagonist this movement towards entrapment: A. C. Bradley noted that reading Othello produces 'feelings of oppression, of confinement to a comparatively narrow world ... the mind is not distended [as in reading *King Lear*]. It is more bound down to the spectacle of noble beings caught in toils from which there is no escape',[30] thus suggesting we identify with Othello's agonized 'demand that demi-devil/ Why he hath thus ensnared my soul and body' (5.2.307–8), having also been ensnared.

Bradley's view of the tragedy coincides with that of Othello himself. For Bradley, Othello's speech of self-exculpation in which he describes himself as 'one not easily jealous but, being wrought,/ Perplexed in the extreme' (5.2.354–5) is a just summary of cause and effect in the play. This would suggest that Iago is the main architect of this domestic, marital and personal destruction. He is literally two-faced, and, in swearing by Janus, the two-headed god of doorways, he establishes himself as the arbiter of liminality, the self-appointed keeper of the play's many thresholds. It may be that this attribution of responsibility is endorsed by the play, but there are suggestions of other factors too. To some extent the hollowness of the domestic sphere is a consequence of Desdemona and Othello's marriage, as discussed in the previous chapters. Their alien 'beast with two backs' (1.1.118–19) is always unhoused, uncivilized, undomesticated.

If the play's opening scene serves to establish the already broached domestic sphere, a number of perverse manœuvres in the final scene act to establish a counter-movement: the re-establishment of a secure idea of the domestic. The last scene of the play answers the first in attempting, repeatedly, the resealing of the perforated space of the domestic: Stallybrass's suggestive concatenation of female chastity, speech and the domestic space is revisited. After the murder of Desdemona, the power of speech is transferred to Emilia, who picks up Desdemona's 'O Lord, Lord, Lord!' with 'my lord, my lord!' (5.2.93–4). 'Imagine it,' wrote director and actor Harley Gran-ville-Barker, 'Desdemona's agonized cry to God, and as the sharp sound of it is slowly stifled, Emilia's voice at the door rising through it, using the same words in another sense. A macabre duet.'[31] Othello is preoccupied that Emilia will enter the room and 'speak' – the word occurs three times in a dozen lines. His line 'Soft, by and by. Let me the curtains draw' (5.2. 113) combines an injunction to silence – 'soft' – with an attempt to reseal and close off the bed curtains. Emilia's response is to call for help: 'I'll make thee known' (5.2.172), and then to ask Iago to contradict Othello's story. In their exchange, husband and wife talk about the right to be heard: 'Go to, charm your tongue', says Iago, to which Emilia smartly replies 'I will not charm my tongue. I am bound to speak' (5.2.190–1). Iago's desperate attempt to keep his plot from unravelling shifts between trying to silence Emilia, and trying to return her home and thus under his control. 'I charge you get you home' (5.2.201), ''Swounds, hold your peace' (5.2.225), 'Be wise and get you home' (5.2.229).

Emilia's reply denies both instructions:

> Good gentlemen, let me have leave to speak:
> 'Tis proper I obey him, but not now.
> Perchance, Iago, I will ne'er go home.

(5.2.202–4)

Emilia's charged 'I will ne'er go home' presages her death, signals her final fatal escape from Iago's thrall and echoes the impossibility of finding a home in the play's preoccupation with displacement and the absent or spoilt domestic sphere. Neither Emilia nor Desdemona can ever return home. Patricia Parker notes this in the context of 'the linking of the O of a woman's secret place with the openness of her mouth', and draws attention usefully to 'the increasingly insistent references to the stopping of women's mouths',[32] but it also needs to be related to the dilated domestic space established from the play's outset. Stopping the mouths of Desdemona and Emilia is related analogically to their sexuality, and to the domestic space that is parodically represented by the curtained bed. When Montano, coming into the scene of the murders, instructs 'come, guard the door without' (5.2.248), he makes a final, belated gesture of closure. But the domestic horse – perhaps that 'Barbary horse' of 1.1.113–14 – has bolted long ago.

This final scene is dominated by the bed. It has been argued that the Folio's stage direction at the beginning of Act 5, Scene 2, 'Enter Othello, and Desdemona in her bed', requires the bed to be pushed in at this point, rather than revealed in the discovery space at the back of the stage. Like the handkerchief, the multiple material and symbolic significances of which are discussed in Chapter 1, the bed is a domestic symbol onto which the play focuses, visually and thematically, at its conclusion. The curtained bed provides a stage-within-a-stage, a miniature, framed theatrical space, just as the theme of jealousy tightens its vicelike grip on the plot and characters. Michael Neill has written of how overdetermined this item of stage business, reserved for the last act, becomes. Noting that *Othello* is strangely preoccupied with offstage action, Neill suggests that 'the real imaginative focus of the action is always the hidden marriage-bed, an inalienably private location, shielded, until the very last scene, from every gaze'.[33] As such, the bed stands as the final perverted remnant of the private sphere that I have been suggesting is sacrificed from the outset of the play. The association of the murder with a perversely sexual consummation has often been suggested through performance. Orson Welles's film shows Othello kissing the breath from Desdemona's lips through the cloth pressed over

70

her face; Olivier's act of murder was described in sexual detail by the Russian critic Alexander Anikst: 'he clasps Desdemona's body, still loved despite his conviction of her guilt, kisses her lips and strangles her, gripping her white neck with his huge black hand. It takes him a long time to strangle her, and all the while he clings to her lips. Then, when all is over, he throws her body on the nuptial bed.'[34] Marowitz unsettlingly elides the elopement of Desdemona and Othello with which Shakespeare's play begins with her murder, opening his *An Othello* with the stage direction 'Desdemona – blonde, white, solitary. From behind, a dark figure approaches. Great black hands encircle her. She yields to them. Cries. Altercation.'[35]

Beds were commonly brought on stage: in their *Dictionary of Stage Directions* Dessen and Thomson suggest there are over 150 examples from the period. Even so, it seems that this bed was a particular source of fascination for one early spectator, Henry Jackson, who saw the King's Men perform *Othello* in Oxford in 1610, where the actors 'drew tears not only by their speech but also by their action. Indeed, Desdemona, though always excellent, moved us especially in her death when, as she lay on her bed, her fact itself implored the pity of the audience.' Jackson goes on to remark on 'the celebrated Desdemona, slayn in our presence by her husband' – implicitly acknowledging the anomalous intrusion of the audience into the private sphere of the bedchamber.[36] This may also concede the audience's uncomfortable culpability in watching, rather than preventing, the violence done to the play's innocent heroine. Iago's voyeuristic taunting of an Othello who would, like the 'supervisor, grossly gape on', and 'behold her topped?' (3.3.400–1), anticipates the position of the spectators in this scene, as the meanings of 'topped' – for which the *OED* includes to snuff out a candle, to finish or complete, to have sex with, and to kill, judicially or privately – coalesce in the witnessed act of murder. James Siemon's discussion of a number of stage representations of Act 5 stresses the characteristic passivity of Desdemonas in this scene: she becomes a prop like the bed, while 'the murder itself becomes the sacrifice of a largely passive victim by a protagonist whose own emotional conflicts are the center of attention'.[37] Julie Hankey quotes the Victorian actor Edwin Booth that 'it is of more importance that Othello's face should be seen than Desdemona's dead body',[38] and feelings of propriety as well as concerns that the focus should not be diverted from the tragic hero at this point have tended to efface Desdemona in her last scene. There are other readings, though: Robert Smallwood, reviewing Trevor Nunn's 1989 production, reports that 'the murder scene was a violent struggle, Desdemona and Othello shouting at each other across the bed, she making frantic attempts to run away, crashing into a locked door, then a chase, their scramble across the bed before he seizes her, flinging her onto the bed and clambering on top of her'.[39]

A textual variant between the 1622 quarto text and the text of the 1623 Folio allows us to develop the final significance of the bed to the themes of tainted domesticity traced in this chapter. Lodovico's final speech focuses on the bodies of Othello and Desdemona. In the Folio he instructs: 'Look on the tragic loading of this bed', and tells Graziano 'keep the house' – an impotent gesture attempting to re-establish or reseal the broached privacy of the fatal bedroom. In the quarto, a slight but semantically significant change replaces 'loading' – with 'lodging'. In seeing the tableau of death as a 'tragic lodging', a place at once transitory and irrevocably permanent, the play mobilises the contradictory senses of conclusiveness and provisionality that are at stake in its negotiations of genre discussed in the next chapter, as well as succeeding to the inevitable logic of its careful depiction of the failure of the domestic from the outset.

4

Tragedy and Comedy

Cinthio's *Hecatommithi* was Shakespeare's major source not only for *Othello* but also for a play almost contemporaneous with the tragedy: *Measure for Measure* (1604). Listed among the comedies in the catalogue to the 1623 Folio, *Measure for Measure* has since been identified with a troubling subgenre variously called 'problem plays' and 'tragicomedy', largely because of the apparent discrepancy between its dark themes of commerce, sexuality and punishment, and its forced 'happy' ending in multiple but coerced marriages. It is helpful to think theoretically about this generic problem. Fredric Jameson has made a useful distinction between genre as 'semantic' – essentially, tonal – and 'syntactic' – essentially, structural. Applying Jameson's terms to *Measure for Measure*, it becomes clear that the difficulty is that his 'semantic' aspect of comic genre, the light-hearted or life-affirming 'spirit of comedy', is absent, while the 'syntactic' structure, the conventional ending with the multiple marriages often seen as constitutive of Shakespearian comedy, is present. Thus *Measure for Measure* is not a comedy in semantic terms – rather its mood is dark, tinged with death and sexual violence – but it is a comedy in syntactic ones – it ends with marriages.[1]

That Shakespeare used Cinthio's story in this context as a structure for self-conscious generic experimentation is clear: *Measure for Measure* works as an attempt to push at the boundaries of comedy, tugging its semantic and syntactic content in different directions to profoundly unsettling effect. This chapter will argue that something similar is going on in *Othello*, a play written when Shakespeare had written a dozen comedies and a bare handful of tragedies. If *Measure for Measure* gives us the semantics of tragedy and the syntax of comedy, in

Othello we see how it is the semantics of comedy and syntax of tragedy that seem to be pulling the play apart. That movement towards division and separation and the play's haunting doubleness, discussed as the hendiadys effect in Chapter 1, amplified in racial terms in Chapter 2, and conceptualized as the interplay between domestic and public in Chapter 3, is here echoed in generic terms. The elements of comedy in the play are various, and many need to be activated in terms of expectations raised by Shakespeare's other plays, those of his contemporaries, and some of the formal antecedents of *Othello*.

First, the leitmotif of *Othello*, sexual jealousy, is a common theme in Shakespeare's plays. In *The Merry Wives of Windsor* (c.1597) Mistress Ford enjoys fanning her husband's causeless jealousy to teach him, along with Falstaff, a lesson. The callow lover Claudio in *Much Ado About Nothing* (c.1598) is tricked by an unconvincing prototype Iago, Don John, into believing his fiancée Hero has dallied with another, and he jilts her at the altar. Only her pretend death and the revelation of Don John's calumny enable the couple to be reunited, in a play that has a number of interesting parallels with *Othello*: the use of a go-between – Don Pedro in *Much Ado*, Cassio in *Othello* – for the initial wooing scene; the stress on unreliable 'ocular proof' (3.3.365), as when Claudio is shown something he mistakenly assumes is Hero at her window talking with another man (interestingly, we the audience do not see this tableau; it is merely reported); the shared camaraderie of soldiers returned bonded from battle and unfamiliar with romance and courtship; both Hero and Desdemona betrayed, unwittingly, by female companions.[2] *Much Ado* and *Merry Wives* predate *Othello* in Shakespeare's career: *Cymbeline* and *The Winter's Tale* postdate it, rewriting the tragedy with a redemptive second half. In *Cymbeline* (1609) Iachimo – his name may suggest a diminutive Iago – pretends that he has slept with Posthumous's wife Innogen, and the cuckolded husband sends his loyal servant Pisanio to kill the adulteress. The servant cannot bring himself to do so, and, after an involved plot in which Innogen dresses as a boy and Posthumous helps defeat the Romans, the couple are reunited. *The Winter's Tale* (1611) grafts onto the tale of King Leontes' unwarranted and self-activated jealousy, which again results in the apparent death of this innocent spouse Hermione, a pastoral sequence by which most of what has been lost is recovered, and husband and wife are brought back together. In all four cases there was never any genuine cause for the men's jealousy; in all four cases the mistake is discovered in time to reconcile the couple; in all four cases jealousy is unpicked and rescinded into comic resolution.

This strong association of male jealousy with the genre of comedy is not simply a Shakespearian trope. In Ben Jonson's *Every Man in his Humour*, a play that lists Shakespeare among its actors at its first performances in 1598, Thorello suspects his wife Biancha of infidelity. There are many parallels with Shakespeare's play, and perhaps 'Thorello' gave Shakespeare the name 'Othello', which is not found in Cinthio's tale nor in any of the other sources. Like Desdemona, Biancha calls Thorello into a meal, and, like Othello, Thorello complains of a headache. At the end of Jonson's play, however, Thorello is brought to see the error of his suspicions, and recognizes the destructive power of jealousy:

> For this I find where jealousy is fed
> Horns in the mind, are worse than on the head.
> See what a drove of horns fly in the air
> Winged with my cleansed and my credulous breath.
> Watch them suspicious eyes, watch where they fall
> See, see, on heads that think they have none at all.[3]

In Thomas Dekker and John Webster's *Westward Ho* (1604) an Italian merchant Justiniano fears that his wife has been unfaithful. The murder of an adulterous wife in a jealous rage is such a cliché that Justiniano can deploy it for savage comic effect: he pretends to have poisoned his unfaithful wife in the knowledge that everyone will believe that this is the standard *crime passionnel*. *Westward Ho*'s popularity can be traced in its sequels the following year, *Eastward Ho* and *Northward Ho*. Here, as in *Much Ado About Nothing* and *The Merry Wives of Windsor*, a comic deployment of the jealousy plot pre-empts the tragic use to which Shakespeare puts the same narrative in *Othello*.

If the theme of jealousy allies *Othello* with comedy, so too does the prominent role of intrigue. It could be argued that a play that is so driven by plotting has more affinities with comic structure than the character-driven narrative associated with tragedy. Alexander Leggatt's discussion of the genre of 'citizen comedy', with which *Othello* shares some features, identifies 'intrigue' as one of its crucial characteristics, and in particular intrigue about the comic threat of adultery. Citizen comedy forms a kind of sociocultural parallel to the form 'domestic tragedy' discussed in the previous chapter. In this type of play, popular in the early years of the seventeenth century and associated with writers such as Middleton, Dekker, Jonson and Marston, the classic triangle of 'seducer, chaste wife and jealous husband'[4] are key to the play's comic complications: in the end, male vanity and suspicion are punctured and female chastity preserved.

If sex is one motor for the comic intrigue plot, another is money, and here Iago's duping of Roderigo – 'thus do I ever make my fool my purse' (1.3.375) is privileged information divulged to us in his first line of soliloquy in the play – also fits a generic pattern associated with comedy rather than tragedy. Here we might parallel Iago with the more obviously comic Sir Toby Belch in *Twelfth Night* (1601): both characters leech money from wealthy gulls, Roderigo and Sir Andrew Aguecheek, keeping them in thrall by promising to smooth their access to a woman. In addition to these comic antecedents, *Othello* makes extensive use of romantic comic motifs. The story of lovers whose relationship is impeded by family, particularly a *senex iratus* or angry father figure, is a common structure for comedy. Greek and Roman New Comedy made extensive use of this narrative, and Shakespeare uses it elsewhere. *A Midsummer Night's Dream* (c.1595), for example, begins with Egeus' apparently implacable opposition to Hermia's marriage to Lysander, and it is the clear generic expectation of the play that this unreasonable parental opposition will somehow be circumvented. Obstructive father figures are another common feature of the city comedies popular in the early years of the seventeenth century.

Thus *Othello*'s first audiences might have been forgiven for seeing the opening of the play at least as, in Jameson's terms, a 'semantic' indication of comedy. As Susan Snyder has written, Act 1 of *Othello* can thus be judged a comedy in miniature, in which the plottings of the villain, the attempted suit of a foolish rival, and the disapproval of an obstructive father cannot prevent a love match between Othello and Desdemona despite their differences of age, colour and status. Act 1, Scene 1 shows us the failed attempt of Iago to intervene in the marriage by tipping off Brabanzio, a small-scale anticipation of the trouble he will go on to cause. At the end of Act 1 the marriage is given authority's blessing by the Duke, and nature gives its own apparent, comedic endorsement in the form of the storm that preserves the couple while scattering the last hurdle to their marital happiness, the Turkish fleet threatening Cyprus. Seen in this structural light, Othello's 'If it were now to die / 'Twere now to be most happy' (2.1.190–1) on the couple's reunion in Cyprus marks the happy ending of the romantic comedy that the play condenses into its opening scenes.[5]

We know, however, that there is more to come, for this ending comes too quickly to be conclusive. And we know, aided by the couple's acknowledgement that such profound happiness is in some sense a source of anxiety – Othello's half-recognition of an 'unknown fate' and the negative syntax of Desdemona's wish that 'the heavens forbid/ But that our loves and comforts should increase/ Even as our days do grow' (2.1.194–6) – that after this 'too much of joy' (2.1.198) the only possible narrative development is towards discontent and discord. Even the moment of perfect happiness is conceptualized in terms of the tragic outcome – death. The tragedy of the play is that it cannot freeze this premature moment of comic resolution.

As well as the comic connection with other vernacular plays, *Othello* draws on continental traditions, particularly the Italian theatre of *commedia dell'arte*. We know that there were occasional visits by Italian troupes to England in the last decades of the sixteenth century. In August 1602 Flaminio Curtese was made an award 'for his charges and pains of himself and certain other Italian Comedians who were commended hither out of France and sithence there coming have showed one of their plays or interludes here at the court on the xxixth day of this month at night', and there are other accounts of *commedia* players in London at the end of the sixteenth century.[6]

Although there is no direct evidence that Shakespeare was exposed to *commedia*, there are a number of suggestive parallels between the form of the Italianate drama and *Othello*. Classic *commedia* plots included lovers (Innamorati) who escape parental control (the elderly father Pantalone) aided by trickster servants (Zani, Pedrolino). A blustering military man 'Capitano' was also often included, sometimes as one of the lovers. It is easy to see Desdemona escaping Pantalone/Brabanzio, Iago as Zani/Brighella, Emilia as Servetta and Othello as corresponding to Capitano. The sense that the characters in *Othello* are to some extent dramatic types is echoed in the unusual listing at the end of the Folio text of the play. Only six plays in the Folio – the majority of them comedies – are concluded with a listing of the major roles as 'The Names of the Actors', and, as we have already seen, the list for *Othello* stresses type characters such as 'the Moore', 'father to Desdemona', 'an Honorable Lieutenant', 'a Villaine', 'a gull'd gentleman', 'a Curtezan'. These types recall *commedia* players, and they also relate to the stock figures – chaste wife, prostitute, usurer, villain, prodigal, citizen-hero – favoured in the city comedies of Middleton, Dekker and Jonson. One critic has argued interestingly that these borrowed type characters give to the play a kind of 'characterological determinism, a profound resistance to the possibilities of free will', and this corresponds interestingly to the idea of tragedy as a more determined and prescribed narrative form than comedy, discussed below.[7] When the Italian director Virginio Puecher took up the play in 1970, he used *commedia*-type characters

> to show that *Othello* is really a hideous game played by the agents of a degenerate society upon an outsider who does not know the rules. In order to emphasise the unwilled, totally artificial and conventional quality of the game, and at the same time to bring home its heartlessness, he set the production in a circus ring, with Shakespeare's insignificant clown elevated to the position of narrator, commentator and shadowy mocker, scraping at an out of tune violin, mingling among the characters.[8]

More specifically, Flaminio Scala's collection of *commedia* stories *Il Teatro della favole rappresentative* published in Venice in 1611 includes 'La Fortuna di Flavio', in which the Venetian merchant Pantalone, served by the witty Pedrolino, opposes the alliance of his daughter Flaminia to Orazio, a Turkish gentleman converted to Christianity. Scala's collection also includes tragedy: one example that may be relevant to *Othello* is 'La forsennata prencipessa', in which a Moorish prince elopes with a Portuguese princess and tragedy ensues.[9]

Closer parallels can be seen when the physical set pieces of *commedia* are examined, since the influence of the genre was more physical than verbal or structural. These *lazzi* or comic routines include a number familiar to readers of *Othello*. *Commedia* pieces enjoyed night scenes and made extensive use of lighted torches for comic effect. Plays often began with the Pantalone figure at his window – just as *Othello* begins with Brabanzio 'above', as the Folio stage direction has it, and calls for 'torches' later in Act 1, Scene 1 and again in Act 1, Scene 2. Perhaps Othello's sonorous 'put out the light, and then put out the light' (5.2.7) registers the final and irreversible tragic co-option of these essentially comic props. *Commedia* 'action would be closely associated with these [stage set] houses, which would offer them opportunities for much comic business in opening and shutting the windows, pushing their way through the doors and utilising the edges of the houses themselves for the purposes of concealed eavesdropping'.[10] The Young Vic production of 1982 directed by David Henry brought out these associations: according to one reviewer, the play 'began with a dumbshow of masked commedia-dell-arte figures acting out, as the program put it, "the abduction of Pantalone's daughter by the black-masked Arlecchino and her suspected seduction by the braggart captain"'.[11] The theme of cuckoldry was also a common *commedia* device. Mel Gordon's catalogue of traditional *lazzi* includes a *lazzo* of unconsciousness – Othello's fit in Act 4, Scene 1, signalled by the Folio's stage direction 'Falls in a traunce', is another notable addition to the source – and a *lazzo* of silence when Pedrolino refuses to speak – which may have its dark counterpart in Iago's final silence: 'from this time forth I never will speak word' (5.2.310).[12]

Commedia involved a good deal of improvised stage business or banter, and there are significant moments when Iago's plotting seems impromptu and opportunistic rather than carefully planned: 'Let me see now' (1.3.384), ' 'Tis here, but yet confused' (2.1.310), 'This is the night/ That either makes me or fordoes me quite' (5.1.130–1). In Trevor Nunn's 1989 production, for example, Ian McKellen as Iago tucked up Cassio in bed after the drinking bout, recoiling when Cassio turns drunkenly and places his leg over Iago's. Later he used the memory of this casual accident to construct for Othello Cassio's nocturnal 'confession' of his affair with Desdemona. Strikingly, these elements of improvisation and the sense of Iago's cleverness are not found in Cinthio's source tale. Improvization is such a key to Iago's success and so contrary to the image he presents to all in the play, with the exception of Roderigo, that he carefully denies he has such skills:

> my invention
> Comes from my pate as birdlime does from frieze –
> It plucks out brains and all.

(2.1.128–30)

Stephen Greenblatt has pointed out that amid this protestation of inability, Iago's simile of 'birdlime', a sticky substance spread on bushes to catch birds for the table, is a 'covert celebration of his power to ensnare others'. Greenblatt writes of the ways in which Iago as 'inventor of comic narrative'[13] embodies the improvisatory power of self-fashioning in the Renaissance period – but he also draws on the prescribed forms of improvisation open to the *zani* figure of *commedia*.

Indeed, a good deal of the comic weight of the story falls onto Iago, and the scenario of the clever self-seeking servant outwitting his master while seeming to work for his good that is common to Plautus' Roman plays. He also draws on the tradition of Vice from medieval morality plays: according to Bernard Spivack, he is 'a figure out of another, older world', 'the laughing, amoral and self-explanatory artificer of ruin',[14] a stock figure from the homiletic drama more akin to comedy than to tragedy. Iago's matey vernacular, his direct addresses to the audience probably delivered downstage, his manipulation and his simulated honesty all ally him to the typical Vice character. Writing at the end of the seventeenth century, Charles Gildon asserted that he had it 'from very good hands that the person that acted Iago was in much esteem for a comedian, which made Shakespeare put several words and expressions into his part ... to make the audience laugh'.[15] The poet W. H. Auden discusses him as a 'practical joker of a peculiarly appalling kind'. In comedy we find 'a class of practical jokes which is aimed at particular individuals with the reformatory intent of de-intoxicating them from their illusions': Auden gives the example of *The Merry Wives of Windsor*. 'The satisfaction of the practical jokes is the look of astonishment on the faces of others when they learn that all the time they were convinced they were thinking and acting on their own initiative, they were actually the puppets of another's will.' *Othello* demonstrates how tragic impotence takes over from comic re-education: the joker Iago has destroyed rather than reformed the victims of the 'projection of his self-hatred'.[16] This image of the practical joker has sometimes been realized on stage: Emrys James's performance in John Barton's 1971 production of what one reviewer called 'the tragi-comedy of Iago' was marked throughout by laughter. 'Enjoying a good laugh almost from the start, James's giggling vulgarian cackled even over the dead bodies in the final moments of the play, and so did some of the audience.'[17] The BBC television *Othello* also ends with the demonic laughter of Iago, played by comic actor Bob Hoskins, as he is led down a long corridor.

The idea that the practical joker steals away the autonomy and agency of his victims' characters shows us a crucial aspect of Iago's arsenal. It is part of his fatal trickery, and his misogyny, to suggest that Desdemona's supposed infidelity is inevitable, to smother comic misunderstanding with tragic inescapability. He suggests to Othello that all Venetian women are tricksy, sexually voracious, and inclined to deceit:

> I know our country disposition well.
> In Venice they do let God see the pranks
> They dare not show their husbands; their best conscience
> Is not to leave't undone, but keep't unknown.

> (3.3.205–8)

Othello's own willingness to believe this suggests that profound distrust of women is the dark flipside of the devotional imagery of his reunion with Desdemona in Cyprus. In Jude Kelly's 1997 production in Washington, Patrick Stewart's Othello pronounced the last two syllables of the abbreviated 'Desdemon' (4.2.43) with particular emphasis, echoing Iago's catalogue of proofs of her guilt chalked up on a blackboard in Act 3, Scene 3, with special underlining of 'demon' in her name.[18] By overlaying the comic possibility that these 'proofs' can be discounted with an insistence that Desdemona's unfaithfulness was always to be expected, Iago drowns the hope of comic resolution as surely as he advises the drowning of 'cats and blind puppies' (1.3.335–6). It is, of course, a supreme irony that Iago, the cool spokesman for self-determination and ruthless autonomy in the play – ' 'Tis in ourselves that we are thus or thus' (1.3.319–20) – should so insistently play on everyone else's apparently deterministic belief in stereotype and inevitability, both about women and about Moors. One of the most fundamental differences between Iago's spirit of perverted comedy and Othello's tragic dignity is in their different approaches to the question of personal agency and autonomy. Iago's philosophy of improvisation, of the mind as a garden to be tended at will, is entirely at odds with Othello's fatalism as he asks 'Who can control his fate?' (5.2.272) and responds to Desdemona's death by blaming 'the very error of the moon' (5.2.118) and the 'ill-starred wench' (5.2.279) herself. Ironically, it is in this tainted spirit of comic extemporizing that Iago supervises the unfolding tragedy. In a fine assessment that links Iago's agency suggestively with that of the playwright, William Hazlitt describes the ensign as

> an amateur of tragedy in real life; and instead of employing his invention on imaginary characters, or long-forgotten incidents, he takes the bolder and more desperate course of getting up his plot at home, casts the principal parts among his nearest friends and connections, and rehearses it in downright earnest, with steady nerves and unabated resolution.[19]

Many of the play's comic strands coalesce in its opening scene, which quotes from *commedia* alongside native festive traditions. The scene outside Brabanzio's house can be seen as aversion of the rough community festivity known as charivari. Charivari, or the skimmington, was a public disturbance designed to protest against a marriage that was publicly disapproved – where there was a particular disparity in age, status or perhaps colour between bride and bridegroom. Randall Cotgrave's dictionary of 1611 defines charivari as 'a public defamation, or traducing of ... hence an infamous (or infaming) ballad sung, by an armed troupe, under the window of an old dotard married, the day before, unto a young wanton, in mockery of them both'.[20] It is an interesting modification of Cotgrave's definition that in the play the disturbance should be aimed at the house of the husband, not the father: Shakespeare seems deliberately to parallel an older Othello 'declined/ Into the vale of years'

(3.3.269–70) with 'this old man' (1.3.78). Iago seems to be activating a skimmington ride – the burlesque procession to shame the unorthodox couple – when he urges Roderigo to 'Call up her father,/ Rouse him, make after him, poison his delight,/ Proclaim him in the streets; incense her kinsmen,' (1.1.67–9), and Roderigo shows his willingness to comply with 'Here is her father's house. I'll call aloud' (1.1.74). Since C. L. Barber's influential study *Shakespeare's Festive Comedy* (first published in 1959), which argues for the relation of the plays to the calendar of holiday and carnival in late-sixteenth-century England, festivity has been a keynote of social and anthropological approaches to the comedies.[21] Again, *Othello* reveals its uneasy proximity to comedy through this interpretative framework. François Laroque has compared Cyprus to the 'greenworld' of the comedies – another space, such as the Forest of Arden in *As You Like It* or Belmont in *The Merchant of Venice* – to which urban or courtly figures retreat. In these other plays the greenworld function is a regenerative space of imaginative personal possibility free from the restrictions of a darker and more hierarchical society: in *Othello* Cyprus is the infernal furnace in which these factors become more pronounced and destructive. Iago, the roistering master of ceremonies, controls the plot, just as he controls its festival moments such as the rousing of Brabanzio from his bed and its echo in the drinking songs rousing Othello from his in Act 2, Scene 3. Laroque writes that, 'just as he is a false physician who uses his art to poison rather than to heal, [Iago] endows the festive role of the fool with a destructive instead of a cathartic function'.[22] Laroque also argues for a collection of images that link the play to the custom of Morris, or Moorish dancing: the begrimed black face, the handkerchief, the mention of 'hobby-horse' (4.1.151). Othello's peremptory interrogation of Emilia mentions Desdemona's 'mask' (4.2.10) – presumably a Venetian carnival mask but here wrested from its festive associations to be sullied with the links to deceit and disguise. Just as Iago uses the celebration of the victory over the Turks as an occasion to turn merriment into violent affray, so *Othello* repeatedly revokes moments of affirmative and comedic communal festivity into tragic isolation.

Indeed, the play generates tragedy from that insistently comic premiss – the discovery and completion of the self through attachment to another. Othello's own story of his courtship and marriage before the Venetian senators casts events as romantic comedy. The romantic narrative of the play is emphasized by the removal of its cast to Cyprus, sacred to the Greek goddess Aphrodite known to the Romans as Venus and thus inescapably associated with erotic love. The marriages that conclude Shakespeare's *As You Like It* or *Much Ado About Nothing*, and the image of the reunited twins Viola and Sebastian, which forms the centrepiece for the final tableau of *Twelfth Night*, can be seen as a celebration of the discovery of the self through partnership – the image of Platonic union. Here in *Othello*, as the discussion of domestic disintegration in the last chapter identified, this image of ideal union is inverted: instead of offering the means for intimate connection with another, romantic love is figured as insufficiency, incompleteness, vulnerability. Othello's autonomy is punctured through love. He is irrevocably weakened by something that should have been the supreme source of strength:

> I fear
> My soul hath her content so absolute
> That not another comfort like to this
> Succeeds in unknown fate.

(2.1.191–4)

Snyder suggests that one 'syntactic' distinction between comedy and tragedy can be found in the relative scope for different potential conclusions: 'tragedy ... moves towards the inevitable, the chain of causality that denies or renders irrelevant all alternatives but one. Comedy always finds an alternative to break the chain'.[23] Seen in this light, *Othello*'s structure again balances comic and tragic possibilities. Unlike many tragedies, the story is not obviously predetermined. Brabanzio's warning 'Look to her, Moor, if thou hast eyes to see./ She has deceived her father, and may thee' (1.3.292–3), for example, rings out as a premonition of doom, but it is not in fact an accurate prophecy: it serves to shape Othello's jealousy rather than to predict it, casting Othello as a mirror of Brabanzio in an obliquely incestuous triangle of father–daughter–lover. Iago's stress on improvisation gives us the illusory sense that things might work out differently, that there is still something provisional about the plot's contours

84

and thus that it may yet be reshaped. Reviewers have often experienced this potential for a different outcome in the theatre. Walter Kerr, writing of James Earl Jones's Othello in New York in the 1960s, noted that 'we are teased toward the indispensable question "Is there a chance, just a chance, it won't happen? *Need* it happen?"'[24] Only, perhaps, when, fortuitously for Iago's plot, Bianca enters with the handkerchief to berate Cassio before the watching Othello, do we see that something larger is on Iago's side and against the comic resolution of the marital misunderstanding. Perhaps this is a racial determinism, as discussed in the first two chapters of this study, a sequence of actions the play finally determines are inexorable because of its troubled response to the marriage of Moor and Venetian and residual essentialist ideas about black savagery. At a similar juncture in his prose story, Cinthio suggests that 'Fortune, it seems, had conspired with the Ensign to bring about the death of the unhappy lady', and his narrator also censures Disdemona's father for her 'name of unlucky augury' (Disdemona means 'unfortunate' in Greek).[25] That hap, or fortune, increases as the play bears on to its conclusion. Desdemona's 'Willow Song', thought by many critics to be introduced in a later reworking of the play, since it is not part of the quarto text, seems both to predict and to express resignation about her fate. Barbary's lover who 'proved mad/ And did forsake her' (4.3.26–7) becomes Othello, even as the 'sycamore' tree puns both on love sickness 'sick-amour' and on the racial 'sick-a-moor'. René Girard argues, discomfortingly, that Desdemona is passive in the face of her murder because of a sinisterly erotic death drive signalled from the outset: 'the tragic outcome fulfils Desdemona's most secret expectation'.[26] Less contentiously, the 1981 BBC Shakespeare film has Desdemona 'at her dressing table meditating on a skull' in an obvious emblematic premonition of death typical of this production's symbolist aesthetic borrowed from Dutch interior painting.[27]

Orson Welles's film structures the play differently so as to suppress this potentially comic narrative. By beginning with the funeral processions of the couple, the inevitability of events is overdetermined. It cannot end differently, because it has already ended. Rather like the Prologue to *Romeo and Juliet*, another Italianate love tragedy with comic elements, in which we are firmly told at the outset that the lovers will die, Welles's

85

visual prologue sequence to his *Othello* pre-empts and dashes the optimism engendered by the play's generic mingling. Other versions of the play, too, make directorial choices that accustom us from the outset to the contours of tragedy. A version produced in Japan in 1992 according to traditional Japanese theatrical conventions, the *Noh Othello*, began with the sleeping Desdemona, represented by a kimono, and a chorus speaking 'put out the light'.[28]

Shakespeare introduces a final cruel twist to the tragic template, a last moment at which the plenitude of comic meanings might yet be activated. Whereas in Cinthio's story the Iago character beats Disdemona to death, Othello chooses to smother her in her bed. Victor Hugo memorably proposed that it is this weapon that finally identifies black Othello with nocturnal darkness: 'Sound this profound thing. Othello is the night, and being night, and wishing to kill, what does he take to slay her with? Poison? The club? The axe? The knife? No, the pillow. To kill is to lull to sleep.'[29] Othello's mind is dwelling on finality: he recognizes that, having snuffed out the light of her life, he cannot, 'should I repent me', find the 'Promethean heat/ That can thy light relume' (5.2.10–13). When Desdemona awakes, he stresses there is a seemingly final exchange, in which Desdemona begs for her life, and Othello utters his conclusive sentence: 'It is too late.' (5.2.92) The stage direction at this point in the Folio is brutal, but apparently misleadingly absolute: 'Smothers her.' In the quarto text there is scarcely more room for provisionality in the instruction 'he stifles her', which may suggest strangling rather than suffocation. But the play revokes its apparent finality here. Is it indeed 'too late'?

Immediately there is a rumpus at the door. Emilia is trying to break into the chamber. In a moment of confusion Othello apparently takes her voice for that of the reviving Desdemona. The quarto text is the more explicable, as Desdemona murmurs 'My lord, my lord, my lord' (a half-line absent in the Folio) as Emilia echoes 'My lord, my lord!' (5.2.93–4). This aural illusion of Desdemona's continuing speech offers the possibility that she may still be alive: 'What noise is this? Not dead? Not yet quite dead?' (5.2.95). This cruel and tantalizing possibility is revisited when Desdemona does indeed revive to speak a few self-abnegatory words. The tragedy gives us one last chance of a comic get-out: 'comedy gets around death ... by presenting it as nonfinal, illusory'[30] – like Hero before her and Hermione in Shakespeare's retelling of an *Othello* more forgiving than this one, Desdemona may not be permanently dead. Perhaps Othello will 'repent me'. Perhaps it is not 'too late'. Perhaps the light can 'relume'. (That this is apparently the first usage of this Latinate coinage, and the only time Shakespeare ever uses the word 'relume', may serve as a lexical reminder of its practical impossibility.) Contrary to the sequence of events in Shakespeare's source, and contrary, as many critics of a literalist bent have noted, to physiological likelihood, Desdemona recovers from her smothering, but she does so only to relapse into real, irrevocable death without further intervention by Othello.

Desdemona's final speeches have been seen as anticlimactic. What has happened to this woman who, like a heroine from romantic comedy, defied convention and her father to marry her chosen husband and to defend her choice among the men of the Venetian senate, is reduced to apparently blaming herself for her murder? The title monologue in a collection of revisionist speeches by 'incensed women' is called 'Desdemona – if you had only spoken!'[31] It gives Desdemona a long, loving speech in which she reminds Othello of their love and counters Iago's poison. Many readers and spectators have wondered why it seems so impossible for Shakespeare's heroine to articulate any opposition to her husband's jealous rage. Perhaps we need to think of this in generic terms. Shakespearian comedy tends to be particularly hospitable to central female protagonists, to Rosalind in *As You Like It* or Beatrice in *Much Ado About Nothing*: women who make their own romantic choices and force their plays into compliance with their marital wishes. Shakespearian tragedy, on the other hand, is punitive. If we look at the roll-call – Ophelia, Gertrude, Cordelia, Regan, Goneril, Lady Macbeth, Lady Macduff, Portia, Lavinia, Tamora, Juliet, Cleopatra – we see that women tend to be the victims of tragedy, whether morally 'deserved' or not. Seen in this light, the silencing of Desdemona, literal in her stifling, metaphoric in the waning of her presence from Act 3 onwards, represents a generic necessity. In Desdemona's final words we can hear comedy's last death rattle, and, in the generic struggle that the play has dramatized, tragedy has triumphed.

Shakespeare therefore builds his tragedy out of the ante-
cedent structural properties associated with comedy. He does
this in part to strengthen the emotional effect of the drama. By
toying with the possibility of resolution, he ratchets up the
impact of the long final act, in which the terrible slow
preparations for Desdemona's death at once augur its inexor-
ableness and seem hopefully to linger, begging for someone to
intervene and stop the murder. Bradley writes that 'nowhere
else in Shakespeare do we hold our breath in such anxiety and
for so long a time'.[32] This argument would suggest that comedy
serves to heighten tragedy through contrast. There is, however,
another possible result of the mingling of comedy and tragedy –
a sense that the black hero is not and cannot be truly tragic, a
sense in which the play at once undermines Othello's tragic
credentials even as it establishes them, that troubling sense in
which the play views the marriage of Othello and Desdemona as
grotesque, a subject of derision and distaste rather than romance
and nobility.

The extent to which Othello, and *Othello*, can be seen as tragic
has long been a source of critical debate. In some ways this maps
onto the debate about race discussed in Chapter 2: can a black
man really be a tragic hero? It also abuts on the questions of
domesticity and scope discussed in Chapter 3. When Othello
justifies himself as 'honourable murderer' (5.2.300), he acknowledges a duality that many critics have tried to reconcile into a
singular: those stressing him as 'honourable' – Bradley,
Gardner, Bayley – are dubbed 'sentimental' by those who stress
'murderer' – particularly T. S. Eliot and F. R. Leavis.[33] Dexter's
production with Laurence Olivier in 1964 internalized Leavis'
argument – which was extensively quoted in the programme
notes. Olivier reported that Othello was 'only a goodish fellow
which had merely fixed the ear-mark of nobility on himself',
and something of the structural consequences of this reading
can be traced in a letter to *The Times* by the critic John Dover
Wilson, who found this Leavisite interpretation agonizing in its
disavowal of tragedy: 'the end was to me, not terrible, but
horrible beyond words.'[34] That an unsympathetic Othello
prompts horror rather than terror, revulsion rather than understanding, is another example of the play's capacity to disconnect,
to frustrate our assumptions about tragic cohesion and about

the nobility of the tragic hero, and, as we have seen from the double title at the outset, its preference for dramatizing and enacting separation and disjunction rather than empathic union. That tiny preposition that articulates the play's subtitle 'Moor of Venice' enacts a simultaneous connection and rejection that affects relationships within the play and our ongoing relationship to it. Iago's prediction of an 'answerable sequestration' (1.3.345) serves as both mode and effect of this troubling, intriguing, disjunctive play.

Notes

INTRODUCTION

1. David Partlett, *The Oxford History of Board Games* (Oxford: Oxford University Press, 1999), 179–80.
2. 'Interview with Ninagawa Yukio', in Minami Ryuta, Ian Carruthers and John Gillies (eds), *Performing Shakespeare in Japan* (Cambridge: Cambridge University Press, 2001), 217.

CHAPTER 1. DOUBLENESS

1. George Puttenham, *Arte of English Poesie* (London, 1589), 147; Alex Preminger and T. V .F. Brogan, *The New Princeton Encyclopedia of Poetry and Poetics* (Princeton: Princeton University Press, 1993), 515.
2. Frank Kermode, *Shakespeare's Language* (London: Allen Lane, Penguin Press, 2000), 169.
3. Ibid. 103.
4. *The Book of common praier, and adminstration of the Sacramentes, and other rites and ceremonies in the Churche of Englande* (1559), section xvi (spelling modernized).
5. G. Wilson Knight, 'The *Othello* Music', in John Wain (ed.), *Othello: A Casebook* (London: Macmillan, 1971), 73.
6. Michael Neill, 'Unproper Beds: Race, Adultery, and the Hideous in *Othello*', *Shakespeare Quarterly*, 40 (1989), 396. He is referring to the article 'Othello's Unconsummated Marriage' by T. G. A. Nelson and Charles Haines, in *Essays in Criticism*, 33 (1983), 1–18.
7. Kenneth Burke, '*Othello*: An Essay to Illustrate a Method', in Susan Snyder (ed.), *Othello: Critical Essays* (New York: Garland, 1988), 129.
8. Jan Kott, *Shakespeare our Contemporary*, 2nd rev. edn (London: Methuen, 1967), 87.
9. David Suchet, in Russell Jackson and Robert Smallwood (eds), *Players of Shakespeare 2: Further Essays on Shakespearean Performance* (Cambridge: Cambridge University Press, 1988), 182.

10. Geoffrey Bullough, *Narrative and Dramatic Sources of Shakespeare VII* (London: Routledge, 1973), 244. Jonathan Bate (ed.), *The Romantics on Shakespeare* (London: Penguin, 1992), 485.

11. Philip Kolin, 'Blackness Made Visible: A Survey of *Othello* in Criticism, on Stage, and on Screen', in Kolin (ed.), *Othello: New Critical Essays* (London: Routledge, 2002), 48.

12. René Girard, *A Theater of Envy: William Shakespeare* (Oxford: Oxford University Press, 1991), 292.

13. Janet Adelman, 'Iago's Alter Ego: Race as Projection in *Othello*', *Shakespeare Quarterly*, 48 (1997), 127.

14. Quoted by Lois Potter, *Shakespeare in Performance: Othello* (Manchester: Manchester University Press, 2002), 165.

15. Lois Potter, 'Agonies of Lucidity', *Times Literary Supplement*, 19 December 1997.

16. See Julie Hankey (ed.), *Plays in Performance: Othello* (Bristol: Bristol Classical Press, 1987), 330.

17. F. R. Leavis, 'Diabolic Intellect and the Noble Hero: A Note on *Othello*' discussed and quoted in Nicholas Potter (ed.), *Shakespeare: Othello. A Reader's Guide to Essential Criticism* (Cambridge: Icon Books, 2000), 120–1.

18. *The Stephen Lawrence Enquiry: Report of an Inquiry by Sir William Macpherson of Cluny* (1999) (available at http://www.archive.official-documents.co.uk/document/cm42/4262/4262.htm), para. 6.34 (accessed 14 January 2004).

19. Coleridge is quoted in Bate (ed.), *The Romantics on Shakespeare*, 483; Lamb in Neill, 'Unproper Beds', 392; A. C. Bradley, *Shakespearean Tragedy* (London: Macmillan, 1904), 164–5; Norman Sanders (ed.), *Othello* (Cambridge: Cambridge University Press, 1984), 14.

20. Charles Marowitz, *An Othello*, in *Open Space Plays*, selected by Charles Marowitz (Harmondsworth: Penguin Books, 1974), 288.

21. Laurie E. Maguire, *Studying Shakespeare: A Guide to the Plays* (Oxford: Blackwell, 2004), 36.

22. Bullough, *Narrative and Dramatic Sources of Shakespeare VII*, 242.

23. Nicholas Potter (ed.), *Shakespeare Othello*, 54.

24. Karen Newman, *Fashioning Femininity and English Renaissance Drama* (Chicago: University of Chicago Press, 1991), 91.

25. Hankey (ed.), *Plays in Performance*, 3.

26. Bullough, *Narrative and Dramatic Sources of Shakespeare VII*, 249.

27. Douglas Bruster, *Drama and the Market in the Age of Shakespeare* (Cambridge: Cambridge University Press, 1992), 83.

28. Michael Neill, 'Changing Places in *Othello*', *Shakespeare Survey*, 37 (1984), 120.

29. Quoted by Virginia Mason Vaughan in *Othello: A Contextual History* (Cambridge: Cambridge University Press, 1994), 225.

30. Ibid. 16–17.
31. Neill, 'Changing Places', 116.
32. Jonathan Bate, 'Othello and the Other', *Times Literary Supplement*, 19 October 2001.
33. Hankey (ed.), *Plays in Performance*, 201.
34. Marowitz, *An Othello*, 300.

CHAPTER 2. RACE AND *OTHELLO*

1. Emily C. Bartels, '*Othello* and Africa: Postcolonialism Reconsidered', *The William and Mary Quarterly*, 3rd ser., 54 (1997), 45.
2. Quoted by Sujata Iyengar in 'White Faces, Blackface: The Production of "Race" in *Othello*', in Philip Kolin (ed.), *Othello: New Critical Essays* (London: Routledge, 2002), 103.
3. Martin Wine, *Othello: Text and Performance* (Basingstoke: Macmillan, 1984), 47; Julie Hankey (ed.), *Plays in Performance: Othello* (Bristol: Bristol Classical Press, 1987), 15, emphasis added.
4. Janet Suzman, 'South Africa in *Othello*', in Jonathan Bate, Jill L. Levenson and Dieter Mehl (eds), *Shakespeare in the Twentieth Century* (Newark: University of Delaware Press; London: Associated University Presses, 1998), 24; Virginia Mason Vaughan, *Othello: A Contextual History* (Cambridge: Cambridge University Press, 1994), 187.
5. Arthur J. Little, ' "An Essence that's Not Seen": The Primal Scene of Racism in *Othello*', *Shakespeare Quarterly*, 44 (1993), 305.
6. John Roche Dasent (ed.), *Acts of the Privy Council of England*, NS 26: 1596–7 (London: Stationery Office, 1902), 16–17, 20–1.
7. E. A. J. Honigmann (ed.), *Othello* (Walton on Thames: Nelson, 1997), 4.
8. Geoffrey Bullough, *Narrative and Dramatic Sources of Shakespeare VII* (London: Routledge, 1973), 248.
9. G. K. Hunter, *Dramatic Identities and Cultural Tradition: Studies in Shakespeare and his Contemporaries* (Liverpool: Liverpool University Press, 1978), 34–5.
10. George Peele, *The Battle of Alcazar*, ed. W. W. Greg (London: Malone Society, 1907), sig.A2 (spelling modernized).
11. Vaughan, *Othello*, 62.
12. Ibid. 53.
13. An extract from Leo Africanus is provided in Andrew Hadfield, *A Routledge Literary Sourcebook on William Shakespeare's 'Othello'* (London: Routledge, 2003), 21–4; John D'Amico, *The Moor in English Renaissance Drama* (Tampa, Fla.: University of South Florida Press, 1991), 63.
14. Karen Newman, *Fashioning Femininity and English Renaissance Drama* (Chicago: University of Chicago Press, 1991), 81; Arthur J. Little, ' "An Essence that's Not Seen": The Primal Scene of Racism in *Othello*',

Shakespeare Quarterly, 44 (1993), 305.

15. Laurie E. Maguire, *Studying Shakespeare: A Guide to the Plays* (Oxford: Blackwell, 2004), 40; Barbara Everett, ' "Spanish" Othello: The Making of Shakespeare's Moor', in Catherine Alexander and Stanley Wells (eds), *Shakespeare and Race* (Cambridge: Cambridge University Press, 2000), 65.

16. Quoted by Vaughan, *Othello*, 26.

17. Jonathan Bate, 'Othello and the Other', *Times Literary Supplement*, 19 Oct. 2001.

18. Kenneth Tynan, quoted in Hankey (ed.), *Plays in Performance*, 253.

19. Jonathan Bate, 'Othello and the Other', *Times Literary Supplement*, 19 Oct. 2001.

20. Charles Marowitz, *An Othello*, in *Open Space Plays*, selected by Charles Marowitz (Harmondsworth: Penguin Books, 1974), 256, 260, 266.

21. Robert Burton, *An Anatomy of Melancholy* (New York: New York Review of Books, 2001), 82; part 3, section 2, mem. 2, subs 2.

22. Quoted in Hankey (ed.), *Plays in Performance*, 18.

23. Martin Orkin, *'Othello* and the "Plain Face" of Racism', *Shakespeare Quarterly*, 38 (1987), 172, 188.

24. In fact, the first black chief constable in the British police force took up his new role at the beginning of 2004.

25. Marowitz, *An Othello*, 295.

26. BBC Race Survey at http://news.bbc.co.uk/hi/english/static/in_depth/uk/2002/race/survey.stm#Relationships (accessed 15 January 2004).

27. Marowitz, *An Othello*, 289.

28. Barbara Everett, ' "Spanish" Othello: The Making of Shakespeare's Moor', in Catherine Alexander and Stanley Wells (eds), *Shakespeare and Race* (Cambridge: Cambridge University Press, 2000), 65.

29. James Agate, *Brief Chronicles: A Survey of the Plays of Shakespeare and the Elizabethans in Actual Performance* (London: Cape, 1943), 287.

30. Hankey (ed.), *Plays in Performance*, 311.

31. Lois Potter, *Shakespeare in Performance: Othello* (Manchester and New York: Manchester University Press, 2002), 31; Barbara Hodgdon, 'Raceing Othello, Re-engendering White-out', in Lynda E. Boose and Richard Burt (eds), *Shakespeare the Movie: Popularizing the Plays on Film, TV, and Video* (London: Routledge, 1997), 23.

32. This occasion, and its significance, are discussed by Lynda E. Boose in ' "The Getting of a Lawful Race": Racial Discourse in Early Modern England and the Unrepresentable Black Woman', in Margo Hendricks and Patricia Parker (eds), *Women, 'Race', and Writing in the Early Modern Period* (London: Routledge, 1992), 51.

33. A. C. Bradley, *Shakespearean Tragedy* (London: Macmillan, 1904), 157.

34. F. R. Leavis, 'Diabolic Intellect and the Noble Hero', in John Wain (ed.), *Shakespeare Othello: A Casebook* (London and Basingstoke:

Macmillan, 1971), 132.

35. Norman Sanders (ed.), *Othello* (Cambridge: Cambridge University Press, 1984), 47.

36. D'Amico, *The Moor in English Renaissance Drama*, 190.

37. Michael Neill, 'Unproper Beds: Race, Adultery, and the Hideous in *Othello*', *Shakespeare Quarterly*, 40 (1989), 393.

38. See Emma Smith, 'Staging Race: *Othello* then and now', *English Review*, 7 (1996), 2–5.

39. Quoted in Andrew Hadfield, *A Routledge Literary Sourcebook on William Shakespeare's 'Othello'* (London: Routledge, 2003), 22.

40. Jonathan Bate (ed.), *The Romantics on Shakespeare* (London: Penguin, 1992), 479.

41. Quoted in Vaughan, *Othello*, 187.

42. Dympna Callaghan, *Shakespeare without Women: Representing Gender and Race on the Renaissance Stage* (London: Routledge, 2000), 79.

43. See Lois Potter, *Shakespeare in Performance*, 30.

44. John Dover Wilson, 'Introduction', in *Othello* (Cambridge: Cambridge University Press, 1966), p. x.

45. Ruth Cowhig, 'Blacks in English Renaissance Drama and the Role of Shakespeare's Othello', in David Dabydeen (ed.), *The Black Presence in English Literature* (Manchester: Manchester University Press, 1985), 25.

46. Hugh Quarshie, 'Second Thoughts about Othello', International Shakespeare Association Occasional Paper No.7 (1999), 5.

47. Craig Herndon, *Washington Post*, 12 Nov. 1997.

48. Sujata Iyengar, 'White Faces, Blackface: The Production of "Race" in *Othello*', in Philip Kolin (ed.), *Othello: New Critical Essays* (London: Routledge, 2002), 123.

49. Dennis Kennedy, *Looking at Shakespeare: A Visual History of Twentieth-Century Performance* (Cambridge: Cambridge University Press, 1993), 269.

CHAPTER 3. THE DOMESTIC SPHERE

1. Geoffrey Bullough, *Narrative and Dramatic Sources of Shakespeare VII* (London: Routledge, 1973), 250.

2. *The Oxford Authors: Sir Philip Sidney*, ed. Katherine Duncan-Jones (Oxford: Oxford University Press, 1989), 230.

3. *Renaissance Drama: An Anthology of Plays and Entertainments*, ed. Arthur F. Kinney (Oxford: Blackwell, 1999), 306.

4. Lena Cowen Orlin, 'Domestic Tragedy: Private Life on the Public Stage', in Arthur F. Kinney (ed.), *A Companion to Renaissance Drama* (Oxford: Blackwell, 2002), 376.

5. A. C. Bradley, *Shakespearean Tragedy* (London: Macmillan, 1904), 146; A.

D. Nuttall, *A New Mimesis: Shakespeare and the Representation of Reality* (London: Methuen, 1983), 133.

6. Brian Vickers (ed.), *Shakespeare: The Critical Heritage*, ii. *1693–1733* (London: Routledge and Kegan Paul, 1974), 27–8.
7. Ibid. 54; Dympna Callaghan, *Women and Gender in Renaissance Tragedy* (Hemel Hempstead: Harvester Wheatsheaf, 1989), 35; George Bernard Shaw, *Our Theatres in the Nineties*, vol. iii (London: Constable, 1931), 332.
8. Stanley Wells, 'Shakespeare Production in England in 1989', *Shakespeare Survey*, 43 (1991), 191–2.
9. Virginia Mason Vaughan, *Othello: A Contextual History* (Cambridge: Cambridge University Press, 1994), 150; quoted Jan Kott, *Shakespeare our Contemporary*, 2nd rev. edn (London: Methuen, 1967), 80.
10. Philip C. Kolin, *Othello: New Critical Essays* (London and New York: Routledge, 2002) 71.
11. Kott, *Shakespeare our Contemporary*, 84.
12. Nuttall, *A New Mimesis*, 134.
13. Peter Stallybrass, 'Patriarchal Territories: The Body Enclosed', in Margaret W. Ferguson, Maureen Quilligan and Nancy J. Vickers (eds), *Rewriting the Renaissance: The Discourse of Sexual Difference in Early Modern Europe* (Chicago: University of Chicago Press, 1986), 126.
14. Kate Aughterson (ed.), *Renaissance Woman: A Sourcebook* (London: Routledge, 1995), 81, 83, 86.
15. Andrew Hadfield, *A Routledge Literary Sourcebook on Shakespeare's Othello* (London: Routledge, 2003), 24.
16. Sigmund Freud, 'The "Uncanny"', in Angela Richards and Albert Dickson (eds), *The Penguin Freud Library*, xiv. *Art and Literature* (London: Penguin, 1990), 339; William Winter, quoted in Julie Hankey (ed.), *Plays in Performance: Othello* (Bristol: Bristol Classical Press, 1987), 1.
17. Freud, 'The "Uncanny"', 340
18. See Hankey (ed.), *Plays in Performance*, 271–2.
19. Freud, 'The "Uncanny"', 347.
20. Ibid. 367.
21. Bullough, *Narrative and Dramatic Sources of Shakespeare VII*, 246.
22. Quoted in Martin Wine, *Othello: Text and Performance* (Basingstoke: Macmillan, 1984), 61.
23. Richard Burt, 'The Love that Dare not Speak Shakespeare's Name: New Shakesqueer Cinema', in Lynda E. Boose and Richard Burt (eds), *Shakespeare the Movie: Popularizing the Plays on Film, TV, and Video* (London: Routledge, 1997), 241.
24. Vaughan, *Othello: A Contextual History*, 55.
25. Hankey (ed.), *Plays in Performance*, 185.

26. Norman Sanders (ed.), *Othello* (Cambridge: Cambridge University Press, 1984), 189; *Othello*, ed. E. A. J. Honigmann (Walton on Thames: Nelson, 1997), 334.

27. Edward Pechter, 'Why should we Call her Whore? Bianca in *Othello*', in Jonathan Bate, Jill L. Levenson, and Dieter Mehl (eds), *Shakespeare in the Twentieth Century* (Newark, Del.: University of Delaware Press; London: Associated University Presses, 1998), 371.

28. Eric Partridge, *Shakespeare's Bawdy*, 3rd edn (London: Routledge and Kegan Paul, 1968), 155.

29. Lynda E. Boose, 'Grossly Gaping Viewers and Jonathan Miller's *Othello*', in Lynda E. Boose and Richard Burt (eds), *Shakespeare the Movie: Popularizing the Plays on Film, TV, and Video* (London and New York: Routledge, 1997), 188.

30. Bradley, *Shakespearean Tragedy*, 146–7.

31. Granville-Barker is quoted in *Othello*, ed. Honigmann, 312.

32. Patricia Parker, *Shakespeare from the Margins: Language, Culture, Context* (Chicago: University of Chicago Press, 1996), 240.

33. Michael Neill, 'Unproper Beds: Race, Adultery, and the Hideous in *Othello*', *Shakespeare Quarterly*, 40 (1989), 396.

34. Quoted in Hankey, *Plays in Performance*, 317.

35. Charles Marowitz, *An Othello*, in *Open Space Plays*, selected by Charles Marowitz (Harmondsworth: Penguin Books, 1974), 259.

36. Quoted in *Othello*, ed. Honigmann, 101.

37. James R. Siemon, ' "Nay, That's Not Next": *Othello*, V. ii. in Performance, 1760–1900', *Shakespeare Quarterly*, 37 (1986), 50.

38. Hankey (ed.), *Plays in Performance*, 307.

39. Robert Smallwood, 'Shakespeare at Stratford-upon-Avon, 1989', *Shakespeare Quarterly*, 43 (1991), 113.

CHAPTER 4. TRAGEDY AND COMEDY

1. Fredric Jameson, 'Magical Narratives: On the Dialectical Use of Genre Criticism', in David Duff (ed.), *Modern Genre Theory* (Harlow: Pearson Education Ltd, 2000), 168.

2. See Emrys Jones, *Scenic Form in Shakespeare* (Oxford: Clarendon Press, 1971), 120–3.

3. Ben Jonson, *Every Man in His Humour*, in *Ben Jonson*, ed. C. H. Herford and Percy Simpson (Oxford: Clarendon Press, 1925–52), iii. 288 (spelling modernized).

4. Alexander Leggatt, *Citizen Comedy in the Age of Shakespeare* (Toronto: University of Toronto Press, 1973), 143.

5. Susan Snyder, *The Comic Matrix of Shakespeare's Tragedies* (Princeton: Princeton University Press, 1979), 73–4.

6. E. K. Chambers, *The Elizabethan Stage.* (Oxford: Clarendon Press, 1945), ii. 261–5.
7. Theresa J. Faherty, *'Othello dell' Arte*: The Presence of *Commedia* in Shakespeare's Tragedy', *Theatre Journal*, 43 (1991), 193.
8. Quoted in Julie Hankey (ed.), *Plays in Performance: Othello* (Bristol: Bristol Classical Press, 1987), 114–15.
9. Allardyce Nicoll, *The World of Harlequin: A Critical Study of the Commedia dell'arte* (Cambridge: Cambridge University Press, 1963), 117.
10. Ibid. 123.
11. Roger Warren, 'Shakespeare in England 1982–3', *Shakespeare Quarterly*, 34 (1983), 338.
12. Mel Gordon, *Lazzi: The Comic Routines of the Commedia dell'arte* (New York: Performing Arts Journal Publications, 1983), 37.
13. Stephen Greenblatt, *Renaissance Self-Fashioning: From More to Shakespeare* (Chicago and London: University of Chicago Press, 1980), 233–4.
14. Bernard Spivack, *Shakespeare and the Allegory of Evil* (New York: Columbia University Press, 1958), 16, 57.
15. Quoted in Brian Vickers (ed.), *Shakespeare: The Critical Heritage*, ii. 1693–1733 (London: Routledge and Kegan Paul, 1974), 68.
16. W. H. Auden, 'The Joker in the Pack', in John Wain (ed.), *Shakespeare Othello: A Casebook* (London: Macmillan, 1971), 205–9.
17. Martin Wine, *Othello: Text and Performance* (Basingstoke: Macmillan, 1984), 63.
18. Lois Potter, *Shakespeare in Performance: Othello* (Manchester: Manchester University Press, 2002), 183.
19. Quoted in Jonathan Bate (ed.), *The Romantics on Shakespeare* (London: Penguin, 1992), 492.
20. Quoted in François Laroque, *Shakespeare's Festive World: Elizabethan Seasonal Entertainment and the Professional Stage* (Cambridge: Cambridge University Press, 1991), 288.
21. C. L. Barber, *Shakespeare's Festive Comedy: A Study of Dramatic Form and its Relation to Social Custom* (Princeton: Princeton University Press, 1959). On charivari and *Othello*, see Michael Bristol, 'Charivari and the Comedy of Abjection in *Othello*', in Lena Cowen Orlin (ed.), *New Casebooks: Othello* (London: Palgrave Macmillan, 2004), 78–102.
22. Laroque, *Shakespeare's Festive World*, 287.
23. Snyder, *The Comic Matrix*, 41.
24. Quoted in Hankey (ed.), *Plays in Performance*, 6.
25. Geoffrey Bullough, *Narrative and Dramatic Sources of Shakespeare VII* (London: Routledge, 1973), 247, 252.
26. René Girard, *A Theater of Envy: William Shakespeare* (Oxford: Oxford University Press, 1991), 293.
27. Lois Potter, *Shakespeare in Performance*, 154.
28. Kuniyoshi Munakata Ueda, 'Some Noh Adaptations of Shakespeare in

English and Japanese', in Ryuta Minami, Ian Carruthers and John Gillies (eds), *Performing Shakespeare in Japan* (Cambridge: Cambridge University Press, 2001), 72–3.
29. Quoted in Jonathan Bate (ed.), *The Romantics on Shakespeare* (London: Penguin, 1992), 496–7.
30. Snyder, *The Comic Matrix*, 41.
31. Eleanor Bron and Christine Brückner, *Desdemona – if you had only spoken* (London: Virago Press, 1992).
32. A. C. Bradley, *Shakespearean Tragedy* (London: Macmillan, 1904), 146.
33. These debates are admirably covered in Nicholas Potter (ed.), *Shakespeare Othello: A Reader's Guide to Essential Criticism* (Cambridge: Icon Books, 2000), especially 132–54.
34. Quoted in Hankey (ed.), *Plays in Performance*, 109–10.

Kott, Jan, *Shakespeare our Contemporary* (London: Methuen, 1965; 2nd rev. edn 1967). Kott's essay 'The Two Paradoxes of *Othello*' gives a grim account of the play as the struggle between the world views exemplified by Iago and Othello.

Maguire, Laurie E., *Studying Shakespeare: A Guide to the Plays* (Oxford: Blackwell, 2004). An unpatronizing and stimulating introduction to Shakespeare, with some interesting ideas on *Othello* and a cover illustration of Saint Iago on a white charger trampling the Moors underfoot.

Mangan, Michael, *A Preface to Shakespeare's Tragedies* (London: Longman, 1991). Accessible and engaging introduction to Shakespearian tragedy in historical and theatrical context, with chapters on *King Lear*, *Hamlet* and *Macbeth* as well as *Othello*.

Newman, Karen, *Fashioning Femininity and English Renaissance Drama* (Chicago: University of Chicago Press, 1991). The essay on *Othello* connects Desdemona and Othello as outsiders to patriarchal order, and traces the way in which the play identifies them both with the idea of the monstrous. It is also reprinted in *Shakespeare's Tragedies: A Guide to Criticism*, ed. Emma Smith (Oxford: Blackwell, 2004).

Orlin, Lena Cowen, *Othello: New Casebooks* (Basingstoke: Palgrave Macmillan, 2004). Compare with John Wain's earlier casebook to see how late-twentieth-century preoccupations have changed the critical discourse on the play.

Potter, Lois, *Shakespeare in Performance: Othello* (Manchester: Manchester University Press, 2002). Stage history of the play focusing in particular on the nineteenth and twentieth centuries, and taking Paul Robeson as the landmark interpretation.

Potter, Nicholas (ed.), *Shakespeare: Othello. A Reader's Guide to Essential Criticism* (Cambridge: Icon Books, 2000). A helpful companion to critical debates from Rymer to the present day that quotes extensively from the critics and offers even-handed commentary on their views.

Vaughan, Virginia Mason, *Othello: A Contextual History* (Cambridge: Cambridge University Press, 1994). Offers historical contexts for different aspects of the play and then discusses a range of stage and film representations.

Wain, John (ed.), *Othello: A Casebook* (London: Macmillan, 1971). Useful collection of mid-century views, including Empson, Auden and Leavis, revealingly silent on the issues of gender and race that have dominated more recent scholarship.

101

Index

Adelman, Janet 13
Africanus, Leo 36, 45, 57
Agate, James 43
Aldridge, Ira 46
Anikst, Alexander 71
Aristotle 50
Auden, W.H. 80–1

Barber, C.L. 83
Bartels, Emily 28
Barton, John 81
Bate, Jonathan 24, 38
Bayley, Harold 88
Best, George 35
Booth, Edwin 13, 71–2
Boswell, James 16
Bradley, A.C. 15, 44, 51, 68, 88
Branagh, Kenneth 1, 62
Braugher, Andre 13
Brooks, Avery 13
Bruster, Douglas 20
Burbage, Richard 41, 46
Burge, Stuart 2
Burke, Kenneth 10
Burt, Richard 62
Burton, Robert 39

Callaghan, Dympna 46, 52
Cleaver, John 55–6
Coleridge, S.T. 12, 15
Commedia dell'arte 77–80, 82
Coryat, Thomas 22
Cotgrave, Randall 82
Cowhig, Ruth 46
Curtese, Flaminio 77

D'Amico, Jack 44
Davies, Andrew 10, 40
Dekker, Thomas 35, 75, 76, 78
Dessen, Alan C. 71
Dexter, John 2, 25, 43, 88
Dod, Richard 55–6

Eliot, T.S. 88
Elizabeth I 31–2
Everett, Barbara 41

Fearon, Ray 46
Finlay, Frank 61–2
Fishburne, Laurence 46
Freud, Sigmund 54, 60

Gardner, Helen 88
Gildon, Charles 80
Girard, René 13, 85
Gordon, Mel 79
Granville-Barker, Harley 69
Greenblatt, Stephen 80

Hakluyt, Richard 35
Hall, Peter 64
Hands, Terry 12
Hankey, Julie 14, 18, 28, 71–2
Harsnett, Samuel 34
Hartwell, Abraham 64
Hazlitt, William 82
Henry, David 79
Heywood, Thomas 34, 51
Honigmann, Ernst 32, 34
Hopkins, Anthony 45
Hoskins, Bob 81
Hugo, Victor 86

102

Irving, Henry 13, 43

Jackson, Henry 71
James I 37
James, Emrys 81
Jameson, Fredric 73, 76, 84
Jentsch, Ernst 60
Johnson, Samuel 16
Jones, James Earl 14, 43, 85
Jonson, Ben 43, 75, 76, 78

Kani, John 28–9, 46
Kean, Edmund 52
Kelly, Jude 14, 47, 81
Kermode, Frank 7
Kerr, Walter 85
King, Martin Luther 2
Knight, G. Wilson 9
Knollys, Richard 37
Kott, Jan 11, 53
Kyd, Thomas 41

Lamb, Charles 15
Laroque, Francis 83
Leavis, F.R. 14, 44, 88
Leggatt, Alexander 75–6
Little, Arthur 31, 36

MacLiammóir, Mícheál 13
McKellen, Ian 79
Maguire, Laurie 16, 37
Marlowe, Christopher 31
Marowitz, Charles 15, 26, 38, 41, 71
Marston, John 76
Mattes, Eva 48
Middleton, Thomas 76, 78
Miller, Jonathan 1, 13, 45, 52–3, 67, 85
Myerscough-Jones, David 52

Neill, Michael 9, 21, 22, 44, 70
Nelson, Tim Blake 10
Neville, John 13
Newman, Karen 18, 36
Nunn, Trevor 21, 36, 52, 59, 72, 79
Nuttall, A.D. 51–2, 53–4, 67

Okri, Ben 28
Olivier, Laurence 2, 38, 39, 43, 44, 61–2, 71, 88
Orkin, Martin 39
Othello
 bed 9, 10, 19, 25, 49–50, 55, 58-63, 69–72, 86
 Cyprus 9, 16, 17, 21, 22, 24–6, 37, 52, 57, 59, 62, 64, 77, 81, 83, 84
 film 1, 2, 10, 12, 13, 27, 40, 43, 45, 52–3, 55, 59, 62, 67, 68, 70–1, 81, 85–6
 gender 2, 22, 26, 51, 54–7, 62–3, 65–6, 69–70, 81–2, 87
 handkerchief 11, 18–20, 52, 59, 60, 61, 67, 70, 83, 85
 historical context 2, 4, 6, 8, 17, 21–2, 28–37, 41, 45, 50–1, 55–8, 64, 71, 74–80, 82-3
 internationally: in Germany 48; in Italy 78; in Japan 1, 86; in South Africa 28–9
 language 2, 4–17, 19–20, 21, 23–4, 26, 28, 29, 34, 40, 41–2, 56, 58, 59, 62–3, 64–9, 71, 72, 80, 81, 86–7, 89
 minor characters: Bianca 18, 20, 59, 62–3, 65–6, 68, 85; Brabanzio 16, 17, 22, 23, 24, 34, 40, 41, 54–5, 56, 57, 58, 61, 67, 77, 78, 79, 82, 83, 84; Cassio 1, 9–10, 11, 12, 18, 20, 21, 27, 36, 38, 41, 42, 49, 58, 59, 60, 63, 64, 65, 68, 74, 79, 85; Duke 17, 22, 23, 24, 40, 42, 57, 77; Emilia 10, 12, 18, 19, 20, 23, 25, 34–5, 42, 49, 59, 61, 64, 66, 69–70, 78, 83, 86; Graziano 49, 57, 72; Lodovico 41, 42, 49, 64, 72; Montano 41, 49, 70; Roderigo 9, 16, 29, 36, 41, 42, 54, 58, 62, 76, 80, 83;
 oxymoron 3, 6–7, 8, 10, 14, 15, 26, 27
 race 1, 6, 13, 14–16, 17, 23, 26,

28–48, 49, 52, 57–8, 64–5, 74,
    81–2, 83, 85, 88
religion 8, 17–18, 25, 35, 37–8,
    48, 56–7, 63, 65–6, 78
sources 8, 12, 16, 20, 21, 34, 49-
    50, 60, 61, 73, 75, 77–80, 82-3,
    85, 86, 87
theatre productions 2, 12, 13–
    14, 15, 18, 21, 25, 28–31, 32,
    36, 37–8, 39, 41, 43, 44–5, 46–
    7, 48, 50–1, 52, 54, 60, 61, 64,
    70, 71, 72, 76, 78, 79, 81, 85,
    86, 88
Turkey 2, 17–18, 22, 23, 24, 25,
    26, 28, 38, 63, 77, 78, 83

Parker, Oliver 1, 10, 12, 27, 55, 62
Parker, Patricia 70
Peacham, Henry 29
Pechter, Edward 66
Peele, George 35
Plummer, Christopher 14
Potter, Lois 14
Powell, Enoch 2
Puecher, Virginio 78
Puttenham, George 6

Quarshie, Hugh 46–8
Quin, James 46

Robeson, Paul 29, 43, 45, 46
Rowland, Samuel 56
Rymer, Thomas 52

Sanders, Norman 15, 44
Scala Flaminio 78
Schlegel, A.W. 45
Scot, Reginald 34
Scott, Hal 13
Shakespeare, William
    Antony and Cleopatra 58, 87; *As
        You Like It* 83, 84, 87;
    Cymbeline 74–5; *Hamlet* 7, 8,
    41, 87; *Julius Caesar* 53; *King
    Lear* 34, 53, 68, 87; *Macbeth*

53; *Measure for Measure* 59,
    65, 73–4; *The Merchant of
    Venice* 4, 35, 39, 55, 83, 87;
    The Merry Wives of Windsor
    74–5, 80–1; *A Midsummer
    Night's Dream* 76; *Much Ado
    About Nothing* 74–5, 84, 87;
    Romeo and Juliet 53, 85, 87;
    The Taming of the Shrew 39,
    51; *Timon of Athens* 58; *Titus
    Andronicus* 12, 29–31, 35, 61,
    87; *Twelfth Night* 76, 84; *The
    Winter's Tale* 12, 74–5, 87
Shaw, George Bernard 52
Sidney, Sir Philip 50
Siemon, James 71
Smallwood, Robert 72
Smith, Henry 56
Smith, Maggie 43
Snyder, Susan 76–7, 84
Spivack, Bernard 80
Stallybrass, Peter 54–5, 69
Stewart, Patrick 47, 81
Suchet, David 12
Suzman, Janet 28–9

Terry, Ellen 43
Thomson, Leslie 71
Tynan, Kenneth 25, 61

Vaughan, Virginia Mason 35, 52
Verdi, Guiseppe 18
Vermeer, Johannes 52–3

Webster, John 75
Webster, Margaret 18
Welles, Orson 13, 40, 43, 68, 70–1,
    85-6
Wells, Stanley 52
White, Willard 46
Wildgruber, Ulrich 48
Wilson, John Dover 46, 88
Wine, Martin 28

Zadek, Peter 48